*P*olitics on the Nets

Wiring the Political Process

Politics on the Nets

▸ **Wiring the Political Process**

Wayne Rash, Jr.

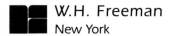

W.H. Freeman
New York

Text designer: Blake M. Logan
Cover designer: Paul Moran/Moran Design Inc.

Library of Congress Cataloging-in-Publication Data

Rash, Wayne Jr.
    Politics on the nets : wiring the political process / Wayne Rash, Jr.
        p.   cm.
    Includes index.
    ISBN 0-7167-8324-X (hardcover)
    1. Political participation—United States—Computer Networks.
2. Communication—Political aspects—United States. 3. Communication in
politics, United States. 4. Internet (Computer network). 5. World Wide Web
(Information retrieval system).
I. Title
KL1764.R38 1997
324'.0282—dc21   96-46740
                                                                CIP

Printed in the United States of America.
First printing 1997, VB

W. H. Freeman and Company
41 Madison Avenue, New York, NY 10010
Houndsmills, Basingstoke RG21 6XS, England

To Carolyn H. Rash
without whom this book would not have been possible

Contents

Preface

I'm writing this preface as I watch the second inauguration of William Jefferson Clinton as President of the United States. There, in the middle of the parade, is a float dedicated to the Internet—a first in inaugural history. While the Clinton administration didn't depend on the Internet or any other electronic service to get itself elected this time, it's still the first time that this new medium has appeared as such a pervasive presence in American politics.

For the first time, a candidate for President has had a well-designed site on the World Wide Web—in fact, all the major candidates had Web sites. Likewise, the existence of the nets has developed into a theme that now flows through the political process. In some campaigns it's a minor presence, and in others it helps win elections, but one way or another, the new medium of the nets is surely there, just as television was surely there at the end of the 1950s, just before the world learned its full effect during the Kennedy-Nixon debates.

Now the nets are beginning their time of ascendancy. By the presidential election in 2000, it will be difficult, if not impossible, to conduct a national or statewide campaign without them. Probably by the 1998 congressional elections, candidates will have begun to learn that it's easier to win with the nets than without them.

So what are these nets that are having such an effect? Mostly, it's the Internet—that global network of networks that has gone from a limited research tool to a world-encompassing means of information transfer in little more than a decade. But the nets are more than just the Internet. In addition, there are the private on-line services such as CompuServe and America Online that have their Internet connections but offer a great deal more besides. The nets include other private services, such as BIX and Delphi, where smaller communities of people with like interests discuss politics and other parts of life and in some cases take effective political action. Meanwhile, spread around the country and the world are thousands of private computer bulletin board services, some available through the Internet but most not available that way, that provide communications to smaller groups that use the freedom of electronic communications to create and carry out their own agendas.

The nets are changing so fast that by the time you read this preface, at least some portion of it will be out of date. America Online is going through the throes of a massive refocusing, and many Internet service providers are finding that competition is a lot stiffer than it looked at first. Meanwhile, the global telecommunications companies, including AT&T and MCI, are themselves entering the world of the nets. All these changes, plus changes in government regulation and the economic model of the nets, will change the details of how business, and thus politics, is conducted on line. None of these changes, however, will turn back the clock. They will only open up new possibilities.

One way or another, the political process will embrace the nets and the instantaneous communications they provide. Somewhere, politicians will learn the lessons of the Kerry campaign in Massachusetts and see that as a medium for tactical communications, the nets are far superior to anything else available for organizing and winning an election. Somewhere else, politicians will learn that the nets can be used strategically, as well. When that happens, the election process will be planned with specific roles for the nets and specific targets among the people that use them.

While this targeting has already started, it's sure to become more accurate, more sophisticated, and more widespread. As more and more people learn that the nets are a valuable resource that's not limited to the elite, either because they learn to look at the World Wide Web on their television screens or because their children are using it in kindergarten, the political process will begin to embrace it and use it effectively.

How long will this take? Probably not long. When a friend told me over lunch a few weeks ago that the definition of an Internet year is one month, he wasn't exaggerating. Things are moving that fast. In the process, the future of politics on the nets is going to be fast paced and, above all, interesting and eventually vital to the way this democracy works. Hang on—it's going to be quite a ride.

Acknowledgments

It's impossible to write a book of this sort alone. Even if it could be done, writing alone wouldn't work, because it's impossible for an author to know everything and have the level of omniscience required. For that reason, I've been very fortunate to have many people who gave willingly of their time, their efforts, and their experience to help me.

No doubt I'll miss someone, and if I do, it means not that my gratitude is any less but only that my memory is suffering as my age gets farther from 40. However, I'll do my best and hope that those I leave out will forgive me.

Key to this book were the many people who agreed to be interviewed. They contributed their words to this effort and helped me learn from their experience. Here's the list.

Democrats

Dick Bell, who headed up the Internet efforts for the Democratic National Committee and the Democratic National Convention; Eric Loeb and Ben Green from Senator Kerry's campaign in Massachusetts; Jock Gill, formerly of the Clinton administration; and Congresswoman Anna Eshoo, who showed me how the potential of the Internet can be used in government at the legislative level.

Republicans

Jon Knisley and Lisa McCormack, who spearheaded the Internet efforts of the Republican National Committee; Anne Gavin, who created and ran the Republican National Convention Web site.

Activists

Jim Warren, who has become a legend as a pioneer of political activism on the nets; Jennifer Engle (or Jen Angel, as she's known to her on-line friends), who shared with me the workings of progressive politics on the nets; Mike Godwin, staff counsel for the Electronic Frontier Foundation, who helped explain the issues from the view of the on-line activist; Tanya Metaksa and Jim Manown of the National Rifle Association, who showed me how the future may look to large and relatively effective national advocacy groups; and Dr. Jerry Pournelle, who showed me what may have been the most effective early use of the nets in politics.

Academics

Mark Bonchek, one of the earliest researchers, who freely shared the results of his research and his thoughts about where his studies would lead; Professor David Farber, who, through his telecommunications research, first helped create the Internet and then helped political users make use of it; Dr. Jerry Mechling, who is taking what the others have learned and turning it into the ultimate end of politics—bringing government to the people. Alyson Behr isn't exactly an academic, but she's an expert in Web page design, and her studies of the effectiveness of the pages in this book helped nail down what works and what doesn't and why.

Everybody else

A number of people helped in the writing process, and many of them did so because of their excitement about the book and their desire to see it succeed. These people included Nancy Tucker of the Army Times Publishing Company and a Web-site spotter of the first order. Another valuable spotter of sites was Mark Eppley, Chairman of Traveling Software, as was Jan Ziff of CyberCasters. Gathering the information was only part of the struggle. My long-suffering partner in life, Carolyn Rash, transcribed all the interviews, tolerated the trips to lonely retreats so that I could write, and helped me keep my spirits up.

The staff at W. H. Freeman was critical, of course, given the relationship that must exist between an author and his publisher. While many people helped more than I have any right to expect, the ones who come to mind first are Richard Bonacci, who helped conceive of the project, helped me believe it was worth doing and could be done, and encouraged me through the steps to completion; Penny Hull, the editor who took what I wrote and made it look good and is probably the finest book editor with whom I've had the pleasure to be associated; and Sloane Lederer, who helped me see the vision of how this book would work in the marketplace.

Finally, there are those who really had no agenda involving the book but who simply found the concept so interesting they wanted to help. They include Catherine King, Public Relations Manager at Gateway 2000, who graciously arranged for me to borrow a Gateway Solo laptop computer so that I could head for quiet locales and write; Louise Vogel, who helped me track down voters in Massachusetts; and Rich Pournelle, formerly of the House Oversight Committee, who helped me understand how Congress uses technology today.

As you might imagine, writing a book when one is a full-time journalist is a trying experience, if only because of the constant interruptions. For this reason, much of the actual writing took place at locations away from the office, where the phone couldn't find me. Two wonderful hostelries were of particular note. When the staffs at The Tides Inn in Irvington, Virginia, and The Homestead in Hot Springs, Virginia, found out what I was up to, they went out of their way to make my life both more pleasant and more productive. It was the sum of little things, from delivering a power strip without being asked to delivering a full-size desk to my suite when they saw the computers being unloaded from my car to delivering coffee during long nights or finding me secluded spots for editing, that helped me create this book. Yes, they were doing their jobs, but in this case, they did a lot more.

I don't know what I'd have done without these people behind me, but I assure you that this would have been a lesser book without them. The thanks and appreciation you may have for the insights in this book should be directed at them. You can send the complaints to me at wrash@mindspring.com.

Wayne Rash, Jr.
Clifton, Virginia
January 1997

scope

dit   View   Go   Bookmarks   Options   Directory   Window   Help

Home   Reload   Open   Print   Find   Stop

Netsite: http://www.democrats.org/

at's New?   What's Cool?   Destinations   Net Search   People   Software

1
N

How Politics, Political Action, and Cyberspace Work Together

It is early morning in White Sands, New Mexico, in 1994, and a cone-shaped rocket rests on a launch pad. Suddenly, a bright light appears at its base, and the rocket, looking more like the paintings that once graced the covers of *Astounding Stories* than a modern spacecraft, rises smoothly upward. In a few seconds, the rocket, which the National Aeronautics and Space Administration calls the DC-X, comes to a stop, and then, balancing on a nearly transparent pillar of light, drifts slowly sideways for three hundred feet, stops again, then descends gradually to a soft landing on a concrete pad. History has just been made.

This rocket, part of an ambitious test program that its backers claim will demonstrate the first truly low-cost way to get into space, owes its existence to the nets—the Internet and a variety of commercial on-line services. By using the nets, a single ad hoc group was able to move information to the people who could do the work that was needed, see that it was handled quickly enough to keep its opponents off balance, and deliver material to the officials they believed needed to see it in a timely manner.

As is the case with most major research projects, the DC-X faced considerable odds, including members of Congress who did not see a potential benefit for another space vehicle, bureaucrats who were threatened by a project they did not create, and companies with a vested interest in expensive means of access to space that feared a new competitor. Any of these forces could have killed this experimental space vehicle at any time, if the backers of the idea of low-cost reusable space access were not always ready and nearly always ahead of the well-entrenched and well-funded political forces that opposed the idea. As a result, despite a series of funding battles, administrative derailing attempts, and sometimes just bad luck, the backers of the DC-X were able to keep the funding flowing and the researchers employed and, eventually, to watch a successful launch.

▶ Politics and Communications

The story of political action is ultimately the story of communications. Without communication between people, there can be no political activity, and the nature of political activity varies according to the type and cost of the means of communications. This is why the First Amendment to the Constitution of the United States includes, among other things, the beginnings of a communications policy. The mandate of a free press is, in its most basic form, an assurance that the information required for a democracy to function can always be transmitted freely.

Of course, in the early 1800s communications meant printing and speaking, and, as a result, the Constitution ensured communications freedom for the technologies available in that day. Since then, communications have moved beyond the printed and spoken word. Now, vast quantities of information flow electronically, from telephones and faxes to e-mail and video, with each means of communications affecting the political process.

As each person adopts a new means of communications, that person uses it in a way that is efficient for their particular purpose. For example, when telephones became widespread, political parties began contacting their officers, workers, and eventually the voters by phone. By the post–World War II period, telephone trees became an important method of organizing party workers and sympathetic voters. The person at the top of the telephone tree calls a specific set of people and conveys a party message; those people then each telephone a set of people below them on the calling list, and so on. Telephone trees can extend for several layers, and they ensure that everyone in an organization is contacted, without requiring any one member to make an unreasonable number of calls.

Telephone trees continue to be major organizing tools as we approach the end of the twentieth century, but other forms of communication have also grown in importance, such as radio broadcasting in the 1930s. Franklin Delano Roosevelt became the first American president to make extensive use of radio as a means of communicating directly with the voters. In Roosevelt's case, radio came at a critical time. In addition to dealing with the Great Depression and World War II, both of which required much contact with voters because of the impact those events had on them, Roosevelt's leadership was complicated by his limited mobility; he had contracted polio in 1921. These factors played a role in his unprecedented use of radio as a political tool as well as a tool of governance.

Eventually, television supplanted radio's role as the primary means by which voters received information about the political process. At first, television was little more than radio with pictures. When news anchormen Chet Huntley and David Brinkley began covering the national conventions of the Republican and Democratic parties in the 1950s, the reports were brief, and the video information was either brief shots of the convention floor or of the anchormen themselves. At the time, more extensive coverage was technically too difficult to use more than occasionally.

During the 1960 presidential election, however, John F. Kennedy and Richard M. Nixon agreed to a series of televised debates, during which the candidates appeared live and answered questions. During the questioning, Nixon appeared ill at ease and was obviously perspiring. Kennedy, on the other hand, appeared poised and comfortable and clearly played to the television camera. What is critical is that the perception of the debate in those days hinged less on what was said by either candidate than on how each candidate handled his appearance on live television. Polls taken at the time indicated that people who heard the debates on radio or read the transcripts in newspapers thought that Nixon had won. Those who saw the debates on television felt sure that Kennedy was the winner.

Ultimately, Kennedy won what turned out to be one of the closest elections in U.S. history. In 1968 Nixon, having learned the lesson of television, came back to win his own time in the White House. More important, however, the political parties learned one of the early lessons of television—that regardless of the content of a speech, the manner in which it is presented on television matters most.

After the Kennedy-Nixon debates, being able to look good on television became a critical issue in politics. Candidates were still required to toe the party line on philosophical issues, but political parties realized that the electorate usually supported those candidates that looked best on television. It should be noted, however, that ideas continued to matter, because even candidates who handled television well did not seem to be able to win unless they also had ideas that resonated with the voters. For example, in the 1994 senatorial election in Virginia, former White House aide and marine Lieutenant Colonel Oliver L. North lost to the incumbent senator, Democrat Charles Robb, despite the fact that North had substantial funding, good television skills (in fact, he was working as a broadcaster at the time), and good name recognition. The difference was that not enough voters responded to his message, despite his electronic appeal.

▶ The Growth of the Nets

In the mid-1970s, a new form of electronic communication began to grow. Now called "cyberspace," at that time there was no specific name for the on-line community—broad collections of people that gathered together on electronic bulletin boards to discuss things that mattered. At the same time, ARPANET, a project of the Department of Defense Advanced Research Projects Agency (ARPA) begun in the 1960s, became generally available to researchers and government users. At first, ARPANET was limited in its capabilities, but administrators soon made space available on the 60,000 medium-to-large-scale computers ARPANET comprises to allow informal discussions between the users of the service. These discussions were organized by topic and took place in the form of messages that were followed by other messages, primarily comments or amplification of the original message.

To get an idea of what these discussions were like, imagine writing a question about a particular topic on a piece of paper and tacking it to a bulletin board in your company lunchroom. As time goes by, other employees see your question and might post their answers to or comments about your question beneath it, eventually forming a chain of discussion that would probably address most questions about the topic.

Over the years, people other than researchers began to use ARPANET, and commercial use of the network grew to the point that it was outstripping use by university organizations and researchers in amount of traffic. The commercial entity became known as the Internet and its informal discussions "newsgroups," and the topics ranged from obscure hobbies to matters of technical and scientific interest. Meanwhile, access to a number of commercial services were added to the Internet, forming a worldwide system that allowed electronic mail (e-mail) communications between services.

Two of the first Internet-based services grew out of early attempts at on-line services. The best known is probably the WELL (an acronym for Whole Earth 'Lectronic Link), started by the founders of the *Whole Earth Catalog.* The other early leader was BIX (Byte Information eXchange), created by *Byte Magazine,* a McGraw-Hill publication. Each of these on-line services encouraged conferencing that was structured in such a way that it minimized the random posts, messages not related to the discussion at hand, and "flame wars," series of messages with immoderate or irrational content that sometimes appeared as on-line postings without regard for other users of the system. (Random posts and flame wars characterized the Internet.) The WELL and BIX services started out with a high degree of quality technical discussion and a great deal of political discussion. Because these services attracted a number of highly educated people, the discussions tended to be conducted at a level above that than was the case elsewhere on line.

Meanwhile, the CompuServe Information Service was growing in Columbus, Ohio. At the beginning of the 1980s, CompuServe was not exactly the largest commercial on-line service; it was for all practical purposes the *only* major service. While there were some early competitors, such as The Source, these eventually were either subsumed by CompuServe or simply disappeared. Later, new services, such as Genie from General Electric, Prodigy from a joint venture between IBM and Sears Roebuck, and America Online, joined the marketplace to compete with CompuServe.

These commercial on-line services shared several common characteristics. Most notable was that they kept a tighter control than the Internet over the nature of discussions. While you might be able to get away with name-calling or libelous statements on the Internet, such messages would rarely see the light of day on the commercial services. This generally higher plane of conversation meant that more users were willing to use the commercial services, which were also relatively expensive. While high charges were necessary to support the personnel required to manage and edit the messages each service added every day, it did tend to discourage participation, because it was fairly easy to generate bills that amounted to hundreds of dollars per month.

What changed the picture of on-line participation was the development of the graphical Internet viewer and the World Wide Web. Together, these technologies made the Internet approachable and the content more useful to more people and provided an easy way for interactive commerce to gain a toehold.

The World Wide Web was started in 1989 at CERN, the European Particle Physics Laboratory in Geneva. The Web was designed as a means of presenting information using a version of the Standard Generalized Markup Language long used in document management. The new version, called Hypertext Markup Language (HTML), allows a document to be created using only textual characters but still appear as a graphical image on the computer displaying the document. Added to this was a means of embedding the addresses of other such documents anywhere on the Internet, which meant that users could see a document page that looked typeset and could also use embedded links to move to other pages if they wished to do so.

Another major change to on-line participation was created at the University of Illinois in Urbana, where the National Center for Supercomputing Applications (NCSA) developed a product called Mosaic, which permits users to view the graphical images presented by HTML files. In addition, Mosaic allows users to point to locations on their computer screen with a mouse pointer and link to another document indicated by an address embedded within a highlighted word or within a graphic image. Because Mosaic was developed by a federally funded development center, the product is available for the cost of downloading it from NCSA's location on the Internet. Essentially, this new concept in computer software is free to anyone who wants it, as is access to the Web sites, except for the charge levied by the Internet access provider. Since many users access the Internet from their businesses, government agencies, or educational institutions, those users usually do not incur charges.

As a result of free or nearly free access to what was viewed as nearly unlimited information, growth on the Internet exploded. This growth prompted the commercial services to create access to the Internet for their members, who then also had access to the World Wide Web. Nearly overnight, millions of people had easy, inexpensive access to vast amounts of information. As might be expected, wherever people went on the Internet, so did their political interests.

▶ The Political Entry into Cyberspace

With millions of people inhabiting cyberspace, you might expect to find a good deal of political discussion and, thus, much political activity. Indeed, the nets are a hotbed of political discussion, and virtually every political entity has some presence on some network. That does not, however, mean that the Internet and the on-line services are favored media for organized political action. In fact, the nets have been an afterthought for many political organizations. While they are being used, they are not the preferred means of getting information to likely voters or of raising funds.

The reason why political parties have shied away from the nets is based on the level of knowledge of party leaders, on the lack of perceived benefit, and on competing requirements for funding. From their perspective, politicians, especially senior elected officials, do not have any reason to embrace the nets. Many of them started their professional careers long before computers were a common part of the workplace and before personal computers graced the desktop. For this reason, they do not tend to have a deep appreciation of the issues and the cultures that involve either the computer industry or the nets, and it is difficult for them to identify with the on-line world.

The users of the nets have contributed to the perception that there is little there for mainstream politicians. Much of the political discussion on the nets is ill-informed, ill-reasoned, and ill-behaved. To a practicing politician, such a world would seem unlikely to yield results worthy of the time spent. Compounding the problem is the fact that some of the fundamental characteristics of the nets make political professionals less likely to take net-based communications as seriously as other forms. These characteristics include the fact that it is sometimes impossible to tell where another person is located, making it difficult to discern whether a person is a constituent or not. In addition, there is the perception that sending electronic mail is so easy and cheap that it can be done without thought, which means that e-mail communications can be ignored.

The problem with electronic mail, which forms the basis for most of the communications on the nets, is potentially the most serious. "It lessens the importance of the communication because it's cheaper," explains Mark Bonchek, a research associate at the Intelligent Information Infrastructure Project at the Massachusetts Institute of Technology's Artificial Intelligence Laboratory. Bonchek directs the political participation project that looks at how the Internet is affecting political activity, political participation, and political process. "It's much easier to send e-mail than write a letter," Bonchek points out, "so if you're a politician and you receive an e-mail message and a handwritten letter, what you're interested in from a politician's standpoint is: 'How likely is either voter going to use their feeling that they have now to make up their mind come election time when they vote for me?'" Bonchek explains that politicians are inclined to associate the costliness of the means of communication with the likelihood of voting. For example, a voter who will willing to spend fifteen dollars to send an overnight letter via Federal Express is perceived as much more serious about an issue than someone who writes a note in a few seconds and sends it by e-mail at little or no cost. The more serious voter, Bonchek notes, is more likely to pursue that decision at election time.

Ultimately, of course, e-mail messages will gain acceptance among politicians. To some extent, that acceptance is already growing. One of the reasons is that most congressional mail is actually handled initially by the staffs of members of the House of Representatives and the Senate, rather than by the elected members directly. Many of these staffers are young and frequently fresh out of college (this has more to do with the current pay scales for congressional staff than any other factor) and have grown up with e-mail as an accepted form of communication. Likewise, White House staff members have been communicating amongst themselves via e-mail for some time. (It was records of some archived e-mail that helped get Oliver North in trouble during the Iran-Contra affair in the 1980s.)

Unfortunately, the problem of location (and thus constituency) remains. There is also the problem of certain identification. Even though a message arrives claiming to be from someone who is a constituent, how is the office that receives it to know that is true? One reason that many senior government officials do not communicate by e-mail is because it is too easy for other people to pretend they are "official" through a process called "spoofing," by which a knowledgeable user sets up an account pretending to be someone else, and then sends mail as if he or she were that person. You can imagine the problems that might be created if someone claiming to be the president sent e-mail affecting policy to members of Congress.

Obviously, the White House can imagine it, too. As Jonathan P. (Jock) Gill explains, that is one reason why President Bill Clinton does not send e-mail to people outside the White House. Gill, a member of the White House Office of Media Affairs during the early years of the Clinton administration, was the person responsible for getting Clinton an e-mail address and, with White House aide Linda Rathbone, for getting the White House on the Internet and the World Wide Web.

"There are actually some advantages to it," Gill explains, describing why the president does not send e-mail, "because pending secure identification of the sender, there are a lot of people out in the world that claim to be BillClinton@whitehouse.gov. And so we do not answer e-mail by e-mail today. We can absolutely say with complete certainty that it is not Bill Clinton. There is absolutely no doubt that if you get a message from Bill Clinton by e-mail it's fake, guaranteed, hands down, no question, because we can say absolutely that the White House absolutely does not do that."

Gill says that the situation will eventually change, however. "When the technology becomes available to readily certify that Bill Clinton and only Bill Clinton sent this message, and only Bill Clinton, president of the United States sent this message, then we will see big changes and that is coming along."

▶ The World Wide Web in Politics

By the time you read this book, many of the Web sites mentioned will have vanished. Unlike more institutionalized services, such as the White House e-mail address, documents that appear on the

Internet related to political campaigns change on a daily basis. Likewise, there is little likelihood that the Web sites of candidates who lost an election will maintain their presence. Because these sites on the World Wide Web are intended to be dynamic documents, when the force that brings them to the Internet ceases to exist, the documents themselves will probably vanish. The reason is simply that it is unlikely that any campaign will spend money on something as out of date as a Web site for a campaign that was lost.

Fortunately, the same cannot be said for the pressure groups and political parties that back the candidates. While the campaign Web sites for Bob Dole and Bill Clinton will be gone in 1997, there will certainly be sites for the Democratic and Republican parties. Likewise, there will be sites for the groups that backed the parties and the candidates, because their efforts to affect government will continue, regardless of which candidate occupies the White House.

Adding to the dynamic nature of Web sites is that for many campaigns the Internet remains a question mark. While national parties have sites on the Internet, they are used primarily as an extension of campaign advertising and public relations efforts. This means that you will see campaign brochure-like material, press releases, clips from speeches and commercials, and probably a response form that enables you to sign up as a volunteer or offer to donate money.

So, if the World Wide Web is not being used to its full extent, and if e-mail is not being well-utilized by candidates and the elected officials, how is the presence of electronic communications going to affect the political process? Right now, the most likely scenario is that the nets will start by expanding what is there now. In other words, the nets will become a prime means of facilitating organization, providing back-channel communications, supporting logistics, and passing material to the ultimate outlets for news and related information.

▶ Politics Beyond Parties

Outside the realm of national parties and national candidates, things are different. For grass-roots organizations, single-issue groups, and ad hoc committees, access to the nets can provide what is essentially an electronic life force that not only makes these groups function well but that may in fact make them possible.

Depending on the group, access to electronic communications can save money and time, increase flexibility, and provide a pathway for organization. With groups that have geographically scattered members, the existence of something like the Internet can provide a way for members to discuss issues of importance to the organization without being constrained by time or distance. Just as in the case of the bulletin board mentioned earlier, group members can read what others have written, make comments, and share their thoughts with everyone else. Because the comments and thoughts remain for everyone to read, the discussion can pass through time without any need for meetings or phone conversations.

This virtual existence is especially useful for single-issue groups, if only because some of them are extremely limited in their membership. Given some time (even a few days) to announce the existence of the group on the Internet or an on-line service, a group can collect the names and e-mail addresses of several potential members. At that point, it becomes worthwhile to create a mailing list, which is an automated means of collecting and distributing e-mail.

For people on the mailing list, these messages work much like the forums of an on-line service or topics on a bulletin board. Even better, they take minimal skill to set up and range in cost from inexpensive to free, and they can be set up so that they add new members and grow automatically. What they do not have is much in the way of visual excitement, but many members of political groups are more interested in the information the e-mail contains than in snazzy graphics.

Other groups use mailing lists differently but still effectively. The National Rifle Association (NRA), for example, maintains a list of its members who request communications by e-mail and then sends out legislative alerts and other notices as the need for them arises. The NRA also maintains lists of journalists who want to receive press releases. These mailing lists, along with the NRA's busy site on the World Wide Web provide an effective means for getting the organization's story out to the press and the public.

Other organizations are less formal but just as effective. When Congress passed the Telecommunications Act of 1996, a number of organizations expressed alarm at some of the restrictions on First Amendment rights. These organizations, including the Electronic Frontier Foundation and the Center for Democracy and Technology, rallied support among civil rights advocates, press organizations, and others to take the government to court to block enforcement of the law. The court activities were widely disseminated on the Internet, interested people and organizations were contacted for support, and, most important, the news media were kept in close touch with the situation.

The result of this active communications was a string of newspaper articles that pointed out the risks of the new law, as well as a growth in support among activists and others. This level of support, in turn, made members of the House and Senate aware of the issues affecting the bill, which eventually led to promises of support for changes in the law. While it is probable that the court actions would have proceeded with or without the publicity the issue received on the Internet, there is little doubt that the activity on the nets contributed to the favorable publicity the opponents of the law received and probably contributed to the appreciation of the problems with the law in Congress.

Other organizations use the nets as a way to publicize their positions, as well as a way to collect information for the consumption of like-minded people. The Web site of the International Workers of the World (IWW) is a good example of such a site. While the IWW Web site contains the basic information about the organization's goals and other items it feels are important, the IWW also uses much of its Web site to provide links to other organizations that share its views. As a result, you can visit the IWW site and from there visit dozens of "progressive" sites all over the world.

Such links are fairly common. During the 1996 presidential campaign, for example, each of the major political parties provided links to its candidate's home page on the Web. The candidates, meanwhile, provided links to the party. In what was apparently a burst of bipartisanship, the Republican National Committee even provided a link to the Web site of the Democratic National Committee, which, interestingly, did not return the favor.

▶ The Net Result

Slowly, politicians and their organizations are realizing that there is value in the on-line community and in the networks they use, partly because it is a form of communications used by millions of people, and politicians know that a certain number of them will vote. In addition, the users of the nets have shown that they are able to deliver results in areas that interest them, such as the communications bill and even earlier legislation and issues. Politicians are also beginning to realize that regardless of the other uses, the nets provide a valuable communications tool that can make their work easier, their dollars go farther, and their operations more efficient.

Other users, of course, cannot be ignored. Researchers are already finding that people who use the Internet and other on-line services are above average in income, are more likely to vote, and are better educated than the population at large. More important, the on-line population is growing rapidly.

Jock Gill explains: "As we move from only 15 percent of the homes to more like 30 percent, then 70 percent of the homes having Internet access, we'll see that people understand that this is really very representative of the whole country." He continues: "In fact, today with 15 percent of the people, roughly, on line already, the demographic research tends to indicate that the people on line are pretty much like the rest of us." Gill points out that some researchers are already saying that cyberspace, as a form of separate existence, may have ceased to exist, if only because it is no longer separate from society as a whole. "Now," Gill says, "it's just like the rest of us."

View Go Bookmarks Options Directory Window Help

Home   Reload   Open Print Find Stop

etsite: http://www.democrats.org/

's New? What's Cool? Destinations Net Search People Software

The Ways
of Cyberspace

The way that political campaigns and politically oriented groups interact with the Internet and other on-line services clearly depends
on the type of group that is doing the interacting and the goals of
that group, both in the immediate sense and over the long term. It is
important to realize, however, that the way interactions take place
also depends to a considerable extent on the way the people who
use the nets perceive the political user. While this may sound obvious, the fact is that on-line perception is greatly different than that
of other media.

There are several factors that are important in dealing with
what Jock Gill, a former member of the White House Office of
Media Affairs, calls the "New Media." These factors control the
means by which the message is delivered and by which it is perceived. When taken as a whole, the result is sufficiently different
from traditional mass media that Gill is justified in using a different
term for the on-line media because the differences demand it.

These are some characteristics that help define the New Media,
as the business end of cyberspace might be called:

- **Interactivity.** The on-line world is inherently interactive. Users
must want to be there, they have to be looking for information

and they are in a position to respond directly to the provider of information once it is received. This interactivity produces what some observers call a "many-to-many" relationship, which is different from the traditional "one-to-many" relationship followed by traditional media.

- **Limited bandwidth.** While it may be interactive, the nets have surprisingly little bandwidth, which means that the amount of information you can receive at any one time is limited, which in turn limits the options of how information is presented. This limited bandwidth has a number of important impacts on communication. First, it makes it more difficult for users of the nets to grasp the full dimension of a statement. Second, it makes transmission of true multimedia information impossible except to a limited number of people who can afford very fast connections to the Internet or an on-line service. Third, it means that there is a limited amount of information that can be presented even with current formats, such as Web pages—if it takes too long to download, people will not bother to look at it.

- **Limited demographics.** Despite Gill's contention that the nets are beginning to be representative of everyone, to date they have not reached that point. A number of studies, such as those being conducted by MIT researcher Mark Bonchek, indicate that the on-line population is currently richer, more male, and better educated than the population at large. From the standpoint of a political organization, these demographics are important, because they can reflect both risks and opportunities for groups that use the nets to get out their story.

- **Location independence.** One reason politicians are lukewarm to using the nets for constituent service is that it is very difficult to tell where someone is physically located. While a person's user name might reflect where their Internet access is located (for example, someone with "virginia.edu" in their domain name is reaching the Internet through the University of Virginia), it tells you nothing about where the person is actually located nor where they reside. As a general rule, unless the government knows exactly where you live, it is tough to get services, although there are exceptions. The Internal Revenue Service, for example, will gladly provide on-line tax forms to all comers.

- **"Netiquette."** Despite the fact that most of the people who use the nets lead normal lives, the fact is that there are different standards of behavior on the Internet and the on-line services from those you might expect elsewhere. Ultimately, most of the rules of etiquette on the nets are based on good sense, but, as is the case with other social mores, the price of violating them can be extreme. For example, something as simple as sending out a mass mailing, which is tolerated when it is paper mail, is a breach of etiquette on the nets, as is typing an e-mail message in all upper case letters (it's interpreted as shouting). Most of these etiquette issues boil down to the issue of limited bandwidth, although in some cases the bandwidth limits that created some issues may have disappeared, leaving just the point of etiquette.

▶ Meeting the Expectations of the Nets

For a political organization to be effective in its use of the nets, it must take advantage of the reality of how the nets are perceived by its users. This means that a presence on the nets must meet the demands indicated above, while telling the candidate or organization's story in a way that is effective for the medium.

A good example existed in the Web pages of the candidates and political parties when the 1996 presidential campaign began in early spring. The first sites to be set up for active campaigning were Republican, as might be expected, given the fact that there was no real competition for the Democratic nomination. The GOP sites were similar in a number of respects. For example, they showed that some time and thought had gone into their design, that the staffs were interested in using new technology, such as Java animation, and that the campaigns were making available traditional material, such as video clips, sound bites, and press clippings.

What was missing from much of the Web-based campaign material of candidates was an appreciation for the interactive nature of the nets. For example, while you could choose the material you wanted to look at, these sites typically failed to include even one e-mail address to ask questions. This meant that if you wanted to know how the candidate felt about an issue that was not displayed on the Web site, you were out of luck, unless you mailed a written letter to the candidate's street address. Although the Republican candidates were using the nets, it was in a way that did not reflect a great deal of understanding of their nature. They were, in the words

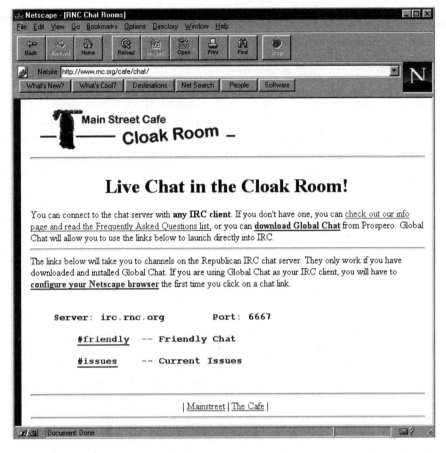

> The Republican National Committee (RNC) was the first of the major political Web sites to embrace interactivity. Managers used such activities as the live chats (shown here), interactive forums, and the public Guest Book to draw Internet users to the RNC site and to give them a reason to come back.

of Mark Bonchek, reverting to a broadcast media model that is not appropriate for the Internet.

In an interesting contrast, the Republican National Committee (RNC) produced a highly interactive approach to its presence on the World Wide Web. Even the opening screen of the RNC home page was different. Avoiding the traditional flags and banners that made other political sites look like campaign posters, the Republican home page used a cartoon of a town square. The idea of the town square was to make the RNC home page more approachable and to highlight the interactivity that the RNC hoped would draw interest. According to Jonathan P. Knisley, electronics communications coordinator for the RNC, the home page was an effort to break the mold followed by other pages. Part of that change in direction included an interactive conferencing area where visitors to the RNC Web site could have on-line conversations with Republican staffers and with each other.

"We're taking a pretty big risk with this," Knisley says of his home page conferencing area. "Suppose someone says something negative about the party or about the candidate?" Knisley says that the party leadership discussed those issues and decided that unless postings by Internet visitors violated the law or the bounds of good taste (such as by using obscenities), the party would allow negative postings to remain. He also says that the belief within the RNC is that the feedback is critical over the long run, and that negative feedback is just as important as positive feedback. "Besides," Knisley adds, "censorship would be contrary to our beliefs and would be bad for our credibility."

As the presidential campaign entered the summer of 1996, the Republicans were the only major party offering a Web site that went beyond the traditional media approach of simply passing out information. In an interesting move, the GOP was also the only party offering a link to the competition. You could click and go directly from the Republican National Committee site to the site for the Democratic National Committee. The DNC, however, did not provide a similar link to the GOP.

In its approach to the World Wide Web, the Democratic National Committee was also modeled on more traditional media. While the DNC site supported limited feedback, in the form of letting Internet users sign up to volunteer or to place themselves on mailing lists, there was no means of interactive communications that compared to the RNC discussion pages. The DNC did, however, provide links to the pages of Democratic candidates, to the White House Web site, to the e-mail addresses of members of Congress and the Senate, to the "Thomas" Web site of the Library of Congress, and to other executive and legislative sites. Unlike the Republicans, however, the Democratic site did not post the e-mail addresses of key staffers in the party itself, nor did it provide a way to ask questions about the party or the candidates. The DNC updated its Web site in June 1996, and it included many of the techniques developed by the Republicans. For example, the DNC site eliminated some of its less professional features (such as its "Hangman" game) and started

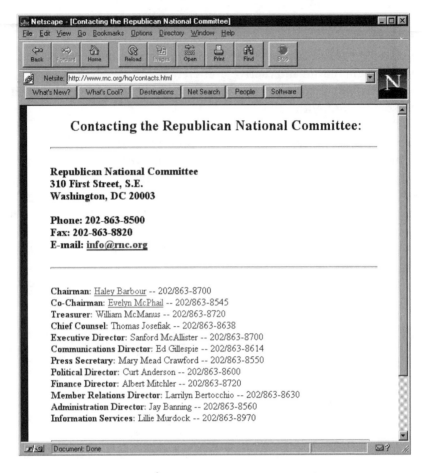

> One feature of the Republican National Committee's Web site was its various levels of interactivity. These included such things as a phone directory of RNC staff, which included e-mail links so that Internet users could easily contact the party leadership. These innovations were the result of requests by users to the RNC site for greater access and interactivity.

taking advantage of the Internet's ability to deliver animation as well as video and audio clips. Soon after that, the Clinton-Gore campaign launched its Web site.

▶ Small Groups Chime In

Of course, sites on the World Wide Web are hardly the playground of only the major parties. In fact, one of the attractions of the Web is that creating and managing a site is within the capabilities of even small groups and individuals. All that is really required is a willingness to learn how to create the pages and a computer to create them. Once an organization has those things, the last requirement is someone willing to host their Web site, and they are then in business. Since many Internet service providers routinely provide a limited amount of space for a minimal charge (or no charge at all) for user Web sites, this requirement is easy to meet.

In fact, small groups and those with unpopular views were among the first to find the Web and begin using it for their communications. These groups had no means of forming if they all had to be in the same physical area, they were often frozen out of traditional media, and their views often were not taken seriously. Because the Internet normally requires a person to actually seek out a Web site, many small groups organized quietly for the benefit of like-minded users and only slowly started to spread their word more publicly. To some extent, that changed in 1995 and 1996 with the advent of truly global search engines, including Alta Vista from Digital Equipment Corporation and HotBot from *Hot Wired* magazine. Both of these services, which are free to users of the Internet, are attempting to index the entire World Wide Web and all the newsgroups. As a result, the entry of a few words can locate even the most obscure items on the Internet in only a few minutes. These powerful new research tools mean that Web sites belonging to small groups are no longer hard to find, and they need not depend on word-of-mouth advertising. Instead, even small groups have a chance to be found and visited by interested Internet users.

Adding to the power of the search tools is the practice of many smaller groups to help each other out by providing links to other Web sites maintained by groups with similar interests. The International Workers of the World, for example, while it contains some information about the IWW, maintains a Web site that largely consists of links to the sites of other groups.

Even major special-interest groups, such as the National Rifle Association, maintain such links, but the NRA's site has a great deal of information about itself compared to most groups, because its legislative and political agenda is both better defined and better funded than most organizations. Of course, the strong funding means that the NRA can afford the staff required to create the Web pages, maintain the on-line content, and communicate with Internet users. The NRA links to other sites are a relatively small portion of its Internet presence.

▶ Browsing Political Sites

Creating links is ultimately the essence of the World Wide Web. In addition to the fact that this part of the Internet produces easy-to-use, graphical screens, it is the links that make the Web what it is. These links, which are represented by text that is highlighted, underlined, or differently colored, contain the address of another Web site, another document on the same Web site, or a location in the document being viewed. When someone using a graphical browser (the program, such as Netscape, used to explore the World Wide Web is called a "browser") places the mouse pointer over a highlighted word and clicks the mouse button, he or she is taken immediately to the items indicated by that word. You might, for example, be visiting the Web site of a political party and see the name of a candidate highlighted. If you click on that name, you will next see the candidate's Web site. This capability to randomly browse the Internet is responsible for much of its popularity. In general, political organizations tend to create links for other sites they wish to support as a way of providing interesting research for visitors to their own site.

There is, however, more to the on-line world than just the World Wide Web, even though you would never guess so from the popular press. In fact, some of the most useful resources for political organizations are not the Web but rather other tools that have existed on the Internet for years. Those tools include such mundane things as e-mail, bulletin boards, and stores of data, as well as newsgroups and conferencing systems.

▶ Checking the Mail

Electronic mail has been on the Internet since the beginning. Originally, e-mail services existed within single computer systems, but eventually companies that created e-mail software agreed on standards for transferring mail between machines, and network e-mail was born. Now, virtually every commercial e-mail system, whether it is available through an on-line service, a company mainframe computer, or on a network server, can trade mail with almost any other system. This nearly global ability to move messages between users means that an organization can be reasonably certain of being able to reach anyone who has access to a computer through e-mail.

When you add this to the fact that electronic mail is fast, cheap, and convenient, these products create a base level of communications that can be counted on to provide reliable, and near-universal, communications. When you couple the ubiquity of e-mail with some of the powerful tools for manipulating and managing it, this old service remains one of the most powerful of net-based tools available to the political process (or most other purposes, for that matter).

The reason it can be so powerful, aside from the ability to simply transfer a message similar to a memo you might write in an office, is that e-mail can also be used as a means to transport nearly anything that can be moved electronically. E-mail messages can enclose binary word-processing files, images, sound and video, and even material from databases. If you wanted to send the final copy of a document to a remote manager for approval, for example, you could send it, complete with the typeface, drawings, and images that would illustrate the printed copy, as an e-mail enclosure.

Adding to the flexibility of e-mail is the ability of a variety of computer applications to create and send electronic mail. For example, users of the Netscape Navigator Web browsing software can select a highlighted option that looks like a link to another page and find that Netscape can invoke its e-mail function so that it can send mail to someone whose e-mail address appears on a Web site. In addition, e-mail packages are widely used that automatically send messages to many users at the same time or that automatically retransmit any message addressed to a mailing list to the members on that list, which allows organizations that need to mail the same message to many recipients to use e-mail. It also allows a use that is functionally similar to a computer bulletin board, without requiring either bulletin board software or the computer that would normally support such a use.

To most people in politics, the uses of a mailing list are obvious. The press office for a candidate might keep a list of the e-mail addresses of reporters covering the campaign so that a press release can be sent electronically, which has the advantage of immediacy for both the press office and the reporter on the other end. It also has the advantage of lowering costs, both because e-mail costs almost nothing to send and it is often easier for the recipient to handle, file, and later retrieve. Of course, reporters who use e-mail find another advantage in that e-mail usually can reach them anywhere, while paper mail tends to pile up on their desks until they return to their offices.

There are many more uses of e-mail and mailing lists than just getting press releases to reporters, although that is an extremely important for most political organizations. Another important use is organizing member activities. According to Tanya Metaksa, executive director of the National Rifle Association Institute for Legislative Action, the organization sends out e-mail legislative alerts to members somewhere every day. In some cases, those alerts may request that members write letters to legislators, that they attend a public hearing, or that they take some other action in an area in which they have expressed interest or that may affect them for another reason, such as the fact that they live in a jurisdiction where an initiative affecting the NRA's interests is being considered.

For political organizations especially, however, the use of mailing lists is not without some risk. As is the case with paper junk mail, users of on-line services and the Internet view unsolicited mailings with annoyance. The difference is that on-line users have a defense against junk mail—they can have their system simply refuse all mail from services known to send out large quantities of unsolicited mail (sending out such mail is "spamming").

If an organization indulges in the practice of sending such unsolicited mail, and as a result is locked out of the e-mail systems of other users, even mail destined for users who want to receive it will not reach the addresses. The nature of the mail directly affects the level of protests and in turn directly affects the frequency with which mail is refused. One well-known case that involved broad-based mailings by lawyers seeking business brought about the practice of locking out offending systems, with the result that lawyers are frequent targets of complaints about spamming. In the views of many observers, however, unsolicited political mailings are not far behind.

The other fairly common risk is that someone will receive the e-mail, change it, and then retransmit it in its changed form. Sometimes, the person who changes and then resends the mailing may pretend to be the part of the organization that created the mail in the first place (this practice of pretending to be someone else is called "spoofing"). Once the changed e-mail begins to circulate, it will be, at minimum, embarrassing. In some cases, especially if the changes appear to be plausible, recipients and the press may take the changed message seriously, hurting the organization's credibility and image.

Automated mailing lists are similar in some ways to the mailing lists used to send out press releases and organization notices, but they usually serve a completely different purpose. The reason is that automated mailing lists use what is called a "list server" that automatically receives any message addressed to it and then readdresses and retransmits the message to the members of the mailing list. Because the mailing list itself can be closely controlled, only members of the list can actually see the messages that are being handled by the list server. When a member of the list receives a message and responds, the response goes back to the list server, which once again sends the message out to the members of the list. In effect, the mailing list then becomes a means of private communications. While anyone can send a message to the list, only the members of the list can receive those messages.

Political organizations like these automated list servers because they permit the organization to create an easily controlled means of group communications. Since the organization is the controller of the list that adds and removes members, the person responsible for the list can make sure that only specific recipients are on the list. The only way for others to see the material that is being mailed out to the list is for one of the existing recipients to specifically send it to them.

The use of these list servers is very popular for organizations that want to keep their activities private. Sometimes this is because they do not want their opposition to know what they are up to until they are ready to let the rest of the world know—a common feature of political activities. In other cases, organizations use list servers because they do not want their day-to-day discussions to become public. Radical organizations on the right and the left have been known to plan their activities as well as discuss their doctrine using list servers.

The biggest danger to using a list server is that conversations the organization thinks are private might not be. Because forwarding of e-mail is extremely easy, anyone on the mailing list can decide to send copies of the e-mail that comes from the list server to anyone they choose. A disgruntled member or even a mistake in setting up an automatic forwarding system can result in the organization's e-mail becoming public.

▶ Conferencing Systems and Bulletin Boards

At first look, conferencing systems are a lot like on-line services. They usually run on computers dedicated to the purpose, contain specialized software intended to make conducting on-line messaging easier, and usually include a variety of specialized services intended to allow users to download files, carry on real-time conversations, or provide access to specialized data. Where they differ from on-line services is primarily in their scope and in the nature of the information they make available for their users.

Bulletin board systems (BBSs) are fairly limited in scope and are direct descendants of the original computer bulletin board developed by Ward Christensen in the late 1980s. These computer bulletin boards are programs that run on personal computers and allow users to create messages for other users to read or to comment on messages left by others. They are usually organized so that the chains or "threads" of conversation are grouped more or less by topic, and each topic typically has a related storage area from which files can be retrieved. BBSs may be connected to the Internet but most are not; instead, they are local operations connected to a few telephone lines.

Conferencing systems are similar to bulletin boards, although their organization is somewhat different, and they usually serve more users. It should be noted, however, that there is considerable gray area between what constitutes a BBS and what constitutes a conferencing system. To some extent, it may hinge on what the operator calls it as much as anything else.

A conferencing system is organized more around the concept of what might be created to serve a physical meeting of conference attendees. Specific parts of the conference may have leaders who control the flow of discussion, while others may simply be a free-flowing conversation. With a computer conferencing system, the model is similar. Some parts of the computer-based conference may be controlled by a moderator who makes sure that messages left for others to read pertain to the topic of the conference before letting them be seen by the conferees. Other areas may be simply general discussion areas, analogous to what you might find during the coffee break in a physical conference—the discussion is still generally related to the topic of the conference, but comments of all sorts are permitted.

One feature of conferencing systems is that they often allow conferees to create their own subtopics as a way to contain a digression. For example, you might find several people who are discussing an upcoming political rally break off to hold a short discussion on who is responsible for buying the doughnuts. Conferencing systems are often part of some other Internet entity, so they may appear as a selection on a Web site, or you might find them by specifically logging onto them, as you might an on-line service. During 1996 Web-based conferencing systems started to grow because of the release of several low-cost software products designed specifically to enable Web owners to incorporate this capability.

To date, conferencing systems have not seen much use in politics, mostly because software for these systems has usually been available only to those who write it themselves, but that is beginning to change with the release of commercial conferencing software. Bulletin board systems are extremely widespread, because the software to run them requires only limited expertise and is often free or low-cost, although commercial software does exist in this area. The political organizations using BBSs runs the gamut from radical groups to the mainstream, but these systems are limited in their reach unless they are accessible through the Internet.

▶ On-Line Services

On-line services resemble bulletin board systems and conferencing systems in some of their functions, but they have expanded greatly beyond either system, are operated as commercial enterprises, and typically have thousands to millions of users. The biggest of them— CompuServe, America Online, the Microsoft Network, Prodigy, and Genie—are household names. Some of the smaller services, including The WELL, Delphi, and BIX, are still home to thousands of users, and there is considerable political activity on all of them.

The difference between on-line services and either the conferencing or bulletin board systems is that the on-line systems are operated as commercial sources of entertainment and information. Users are charged for admission, the people who operate and maintain the systems are paid, there is usually worldwide access, and, while they all have access to (and sometimes from) the Internet, it is a sideline rather than the reason for their existence. The messages that appear in the forum areas on these services are monitored for content and objectionable messages are deleted.

The on-line services attract so many people because they are typically designed to be easy to use for their intended audience, and the audience has some assurance that it will not be exposed to truly offensive material. Both America Online and CompuServe recruit members by sending out free copies of their access software and offering free access time for potential customers to get used to their service. Microsoft includes its access software as a part of Windows 95. Many people find the offer of free software with a nonintimidating interface enticing enough to use the on-line services at least occasionally. As a result, users of these services represent broad demographics for the on-line services.

The huge numbers and the broad demographics make the commercial on-line services very attractive for mainstream political organizations. The major parties have their presence on-line, as do some major lobbying groups and many candidates. During Bill Clinton's 1992 campaign, for example, his initial net-based presence was conducted by Jock Gill using America Online.

Political activities on the on-line services, however, go beyond formal activities by candidates and political organizations. Each of the on-line services has groups of forums in which users can discuss politics among themselves. These forums may be aimed at specific interests, such as women's or senior's issues, or they may be aimed at specific events or trends. The details depend on the service and to some extent on the desires of the person managing the forum.

While the political organizations do not necessarily control the forums on these services, they can still be useful means of communication. Many organizations appoint a staffer or a volunteer to monitor specific forums, either as a way to spot trends and issues or as a way to make sure that the organization's goals and actions are not being misrepresented. While not every organization or campaign pays attention to the on-line services and some do not acknowledge their activities, the forums do provide input for the organizations that use them.

Because many of the on-line services will create private forums for groups, these services are also the home to a number of small pressure groups and even some ad hoc political groups. Many of these groups, which form to deal with a specific situation or a single issue, are small enough that they need to meet on-line if they are to exist at all. Others are transnational groups that cover so many continents and time zones that physical meetings are nearly impossible, despite their numbers.

The group that was instrumental in securing funding for the DC-X rocket described at the beginning of Chapter 1 was such a group and met for years solely as an on-line presence. Working in conjunction with other space advocacy groups, this ad hoc group (scientists, military officers, bureaucrats, congressional staffers, and members of advocacy groups) used BIX, starting when it still belonged to *Byte Magazine*, to produce position papers, plan strategy, and coordinate meetings and sometimes find ways to apply pressure to members of Congress controlling the process.

Meanwhile, other space advocacy groups, including the National Space Society, used other on-line services to the same end, as well as to plan briefings and information sessions and more formal lobbying activities. As a result of the communications provided by the on-line services, these groups were able to react much more quickly than they might have otherwise and were able to head off attempts to short circuit the program and to ensure that funding was delivered to keep the project alive.

▶ All the News

The Internet newsgroups, on the surface, resemble the forums and conferences on other systems, but there are some significant differences, most notably that most newsgroups are not moderated, which means no specific person or group is responsible for their content. While there are a few moderated newsgroups, for the most part the content issue is handled by peer pressure, which means that messages that are grossly off topic are subject to derision and name-calling, but little else.

If the idea of controlling content through name-calling seems dubious, it is still an important part of the Internet. In fact, the newsgroups, of which there may be more than 20,000 (the number changes daily), may have a message base larger than all of the on-line services combined. In addition, many of the newsgroups attract users with a great deal of knowledge, so their uncontrolled nature does not mean they lack information.

Unfortunately, the newsgroups have also attracted attention as one of the many homes of pornographic photos and stories, as a place in which other unsavory practices and discussions take place, and as the place where much pirated software is traded. The political discussions that take place in the newsgroups are many, but the information can be hard to find and much of it is unfocused.

The nature of the newsgroups makes them hard to manage for many but not all political purposes. For example, when users of the nets were working to overturn the Communications Decency Act (incorporated into the Telecommunications Act of 1996), the newsgroups provided an important base from which to form strategy, collect support, and try out arguments. While many groups might be hard pressed to use the newsgroups, others use them as a source for ideas and concerns, especially among the communities that use the Internet, and as a way to judge the value of concepts that may resonate with users of the nets.

▶ Chatting the Night Away

At first look, the chat services seem unlikely to be of much benefit to a political organization, but that is not the case at all. In fact, chat services provide a useful way for an organization to get some publicity and voter contact at little risk, and they can provide a means of input for the specific communities that frequent on-line services. The details of these services vary according to whether they are being run by an on-line service or over the Internet as part of the Internet Relay Chat (IRC) service. Like the newsgroups and forums on the Internet and the on-line services, the amount of control depends on the service and the subject under discussion. Also like the newsgroups, the chat services have gained a somewhat unsavory reputation, because they have been used to lure young children into contact with child abusers.

To some extent, the chat services do not deserve the reputation they have gained. While there have been some incidents could have been prevented, the on-line services go to great lengths to monitor the conversations as they take place and try to prevent the unfortunate situations reported by the media.

In fact, the chat services on the commercial on-line services are regularly used as a way to provide a limited sort of discussion between a public figure and the members of the service hosting the chat session. To use these sessions, members type their questions, which are then seen by other people participating in the chat session. If the session is hosting a special guest, then the questions are aimed at the guest for responses.

Because the interaction in the chat session is a form of written communication, the person preparing the answers can make sure that their position is stated clearly. Likewise, the person submitting the question can be assured that it will be transmitted clearly. While typing speeds are such that only limited information can be covered during a chat session of reasonable length, these sessions are proving extremely popular among users of commercial services. More important, the somewhat controlled nature of chat sessions has made them popular for the guests as well, who report that they feel that they can get their word out without having it filtered or turned into sound bites.

The IRC service on the Internet works in much the same way as the chat sessions of the on-line services. The biggest difference is that there are few limitations and, like the newsgroups, pretty much anything goes. On the other hand, the IRCs can attract thousands of Internet users and can produce useful input despite their lack of control.

▶ File Libraries and FTP Sites

While they do not capture the imagination of the media or the public as much as the graphical Web sites, file libraries can be one of the most practical political assets available on the nets. Regardless of what you might call them, these collections of files are available for people to transfer to their computers for later reading, reference, or study. Because all services as well as the Internet support the transfer of binary files (such as the ones used by most word processors) and images, this means that such a service can provide nearly anything that can be stored on a computer.

The means by which these libraries of files are handled differs greatly, with the details depending on the service and the software used to retrieve the files. In the case of on-line services, such as America Online and CompuServe, transferring a file from the service to your computer requires that you request access to the file libraries, which are separate collections of menus that indicate what files are available, then read the descriptions and indicate which one you want to transfer to your computer (or download, as experienced net hands call it).

With the Internet, things are usually a lot easier. Internet-based services support the File Transfer Protocol (FTP), which allows you to request the same type of files you can get with the other service. What is different is that most Web browsers are capable of telling when the remote site is attempting to use FTP and then accepting a file using that means. In fact, many Web pages support file transfers by setting up links directly to files that can be received using FTP. For example, you can read about a speech on a candidate's Web site, then click your mouse pointer on a link and have the text of the speech transferred to your computer for later study.

▶ Multimedia Services

Most of the development in multimedia services is taking place on the Web, partly because most commercial on-line services use proprietary software that makes adding a new capability somewhat difficult, and partly because even fewer users of the on-line services have fast connections. On the Internet, at least, people with university, government, and corporate accounts may have high-speed access to the Internet during business hours, and there is a growing number of people with ISDN (a special kind of phone line using the Integrated Services Digital Network for high speed digital connections) access to the Internet.

These faster connections allow Web site operators to produce program material that includes live audio feeds and recorded audio and video material. You could, for example, transmit the nomination speeches from the political conventions live over the Internet using software such as RealAudio from Progressive Networks, Inc. (Seattle, Washington). This software allows a source of audio to be fed into the sound card on a computer, and then transmitted as a stream of encoded audio to anyone who wants to listen. The software required for decoding the audio feeds is provided free by the companies that produce the server software.

Video feeds are more difficult to accomplish, because video requires more bandwidth. Currently, most video transmission is very low resolution with a slow frame rate, so it is not about to challenge broadcast television. On the other hand, considerable work is being done to find ways to feed at least low-resolution video across the Internet at reasonable frame rates, so that before long video could also be a useful part of the Internet tool kit.

▶ Finding the Right Model

To a considerable extent, success in using the on-line services or the Internet depends on learning how best to interact with the service and the users of the service. Part of the problem is getting past the old way of doing things, such as simply providing a central source for transmitting information. According to MIT researcher Mark Bonchek, this way of doing things is not particularly effective. He believes that political organizations should be looking at something else.

"Here is a completely different medium," Bonchek says. "You have the opportunity to narrowcast [send specific information to specific people, as opposed to the 'broadcast' of general information to everyone]; you can send a different message to different groups of people. You can create a two-way flow of information." Bonchek also says that with the nets, organizations can have a form of group communication that is impossible with traditional media and adds that this delay in getting used to a new medium has happened before. He compares it to the first television newscasts, which were very much like radio newscasts, except that they showed an image of the newscaster reading the news.

The difference, says Bonchek, is that on-line communications do not involve an audience in the way that traditional media have viewers and readers. Instead, the new media follow what Bonchek calls a network model. "There is no audience there," he says. "Everybody is a participant, and that's the way to think about it."

File View Go Bookmarks Options Directory Window Help

Home   Reload   Open   Print   Find   Shop

Netsite: http://www.democrats.org/

What's New?   What's Cool?   Destinations   Net Search   People   Software

*T*raditional

Politics

"People in politics are much more conservative than people outside politics realize," says Dick Bell, interactive media director for the Democratic National Committee Communications Department. "This is not a business where if you make a bad decision you lose 5 percent market share. It's an all or nothing business." In that statement Bell explains why the mainstream political parties are moving relatively slowly in adopting on-line technology for use in campaigns. The problem, as Bell and others see it, is that political campaigns cannot afford the risk of trying something unproved, unless they have no other choice or are forced into it by some other action.

This problem is one of the primary areas in which political parties fundamentally differ from private businesses. Because there is no prize for second place in elections, parties and campaign staffs want to be certain that every dollar they spend and every resource they allocate will contribute to winning, and, at the same time, they want to make sure that risk is avoided wherever possible.

"And so, people who run this business are always looking over their shoulders at what worked last time," Bell continues. "Once you've been through a couple of election cycles you will notice that whoever happens to win in a given cycle, they become the people

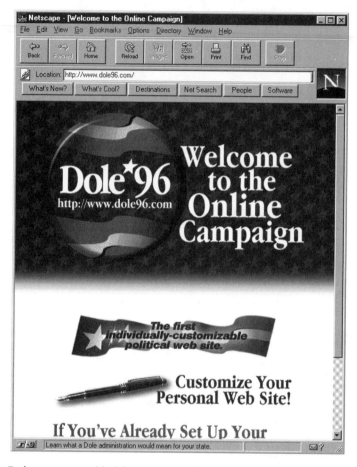

> The Dole campaign added features that allowed visitors to customize their Dole home page, which allowed the Dole Internet site to present items of interest to return visitors.

who do this sort of talk circuit of political consultants about what worked."

During the 1996 presidential campaign, there was no track record to show what worked on the nets, and, as a result, the candidates and parties that could afford to take risks (or who had to take risks to gain a perceived edge) showed innovation on line. In 1996 this frequently meant that the Republican Party set the standard for on-line activity, especially on the Internet.

Because the Democratic Party had the incumbent as its candidate, the Republicans had an additional incentive to use innovative methods in a competitive, and at times bruising, series of primaries. While the eventual party nominee, Kansas Senator Robert Dole, was assumed by many to have the best shot at winning most of the primaries, there was sufficient doubt that other contenders, notably former commentator Patrick Buchanan and publisher Steve Forbes, were able to mount aggressive campaigns. In such cases, candidates and their staffs looked for every available edge, especially when it came to getting their stories to the news media.

The result of the demand for an edge and for a path to the media led to quick moves to establish an on-line presence by the major contenders by the time active campaigning began for the February 1996 New Hampshire primaries. In the case of New Hampshire, the candidates were encouraged by the presence of several heavily used sites on the World Wide Web devoted to the election. These sites were already providing links to each candidate, with the result that they effectively funneled Internet users into the candidates sites.

Adding to the interest was the fact that these same Web sites were also favorite stops for the news media. One television station in Manchester, for example, created a Web site devoted exclusively to that state's primary elections and provided access to the existing Web sites of every candidate in the primary.

Initially, the Web sites of the candidates were little more than electronic versions of their existing campaign literature. Soon, however, campaign staffs began posting point papers, position documents, and press releases on their Internet sites. This additional information, plus the fact that candidate sites were being listed on the major Internet index sites, resulted in additional traffic on Web sites that had useful content, which in turn led to more improvements.

Patrick Buchanan's campaign was one of the first to add some interactive capabilities to its Internet site. The Buchanan Web site began to solicit the names of potential volunteers and donors, and it provided a search service so that visitors to the site could find the candidate's position on any topic in seconds. By the day of the New Hampshire primary, the Buchanan site was more interactive than those of the other Republican candidates.

Meanwhile, the Democratic Party presidential candidates were nowhere to be found. The reason was, as Bell suggests, that it was not worth the risk or expense, because Bill Clinton had no serious opposition and was going to win anyway. Coupled with the fact that as the sitting president of the United States, Clinton had nearly unlimited access to the media, there was simply no reason for the Clinton campaign to go on line.

▶ The National Committees

"The primary purpose of the on-line presence has been to communicate the Democratic message to people in the on-line community," explains Bell. "If there is a historical complaint in almost every political organization that I have ever worked with, it is that whoever is in the level above doesn't share enough information." Bell also says that use of on-line communications allows the party to flatten the organization's information flow and in the process provide information to everyone that used to go only to limited distribution lists or to party headquarters staff.

Because of the need for better communications, the Democratic National Committee began setting up its permanent on-line presence early in 1995. This presence, which was a site on the World Wide Web, was based on experience the party had during the 1992 presidential campaign, in which Jock Gill, then a staffer on the Clinton campaign and later in the White House, started the first e-mail–based activities on America Online. Gill was active in providing information to the news media and others through electronic mail and was instrumental in getting the White House on line with e-mail and eventually an official page on the Internet.

At the Republican National Committee things took longer to get started, but in part that was because staffers there wanted to see how the Democrats did and partly because the RNC wanted to target its site carefully before launch.

"The Republican Party was nowhere on the Internet in 1992, when Bush ran," says Lisa McCormack, director of publications and on-line communications for the Republican National Committee. "We spent six months really looking into it." McCormack adds, "It's a way of communicating with our grass roots, which is a huge priority." McCormack, like Bell, also notes that the RNC felt it was important to make sure that the party's views were accurately reflected to the on-line community, rather than being filtered through news reports or other services on the Internet. She also felt that the Republican stand on issues would be attractive to the on-line community. "When you express your stand on issues, and why you believe what you believe in, then others will follow,"

McCormack says, explaining that it is in effect describing the Republican Party to people who may never have had first-hand exposure. "We feel that the demographics of the Internet lean towards the Republican Party's demographics."

Once the decision was made to create a presence on the Internet, McCormack studied sites, both political and nonpolitical, that she felt were effective in getting their message across. "While we were studying it, the DNC came up with their site," McCormack says, describing the process that led the RNC onto the Internet. "There was some gnashing of teeth over here at the RNC." McCormack says that the competition between the party Web sites began to feel like the space race that began after the Soviet Union launched Sputnik. Instead of rushing, however, the RNC decided to study the Democrat sites and then move deliberately. "We'll just make sure it's a better mouse trap," McCormack recalls of the conversations at the time.

The Democrats, meanwhile, were aiming at getting the word out as well, and with as few filters as possible. "People on line want to disintermediate [remove intermediaries]," Bell says, explaining how the party chose the information for its sites and presentation of its Internet activities. "They want direct access to information." Bell adds, "We'd rather let them read our materials unfiltered."

Another primary consideration for the Democratic Party was the press, which in 1995 was well on its way to adopting computer-assisted reporting as a way to cope with chronic budget and staff shortages. Bell realized that the DNC could provide information on line for the media and that the result could be better coverage. "I notice a very clear use by the media of the materials we put out," Bell says, explaining that reporters tend to prefer the easiest course to getting information wherever possible. "It's a lot easier to get this stuff in your e-mail box, for example, than it is to have to wait for a fax or sort through the fax pile in your office," Bell explains.

▶ Who Owns the Audience?

While reaching the media and the members of a campaign staff are very important, ultimately the major goal of any political party presence on line is to attract voters. Both parties feel that the people who use the Internet and the on-line services are an ideal target. Interestingly, however, both parties list almost the same qualities of on-line users as reasons why their respective parties will have more appeal.

In Lisa McCormack's view, there are actually two different users. "First of all," she notes, the typical user on the nets is, "intelligent, self-sufficient, confident, curious, and likes a good strong argument—they would like an argument just for the sake and the joy, because there is a joy to arguing. Resourceful, so in that sense, independent." They would have "a better than average education. Certainly has had at least two years of college, and probably would not mind the idea of going into business for themselves. You know it's sort of that confident kind of entrepreneurial person who isn't afraid of life, likes to be challenged." McCormack also suggests that, above all, the typical user displays a great curiosity, because such an activity defines one of the popular pastimes on the net—browsing for information.

"It's like going into the world's greatest library. You think of the Library of Alexandria, as it was described in the history books. God, I would have loved to have visited there, and now we, in a certain sense, have the ultimate Library of Alexandria. We have the Internet, we have the Web, and it's just wondrous when you consider it."

The other type of user, McCormack says, is younger. "I would say mid-twenties, a bit of a smart ass, cocky but sociable, likes people. You can see it when you read the discussion groups and stuff. Likes other people, because Internet is connecting with one another and has disposable income because even if he or she uses the computer for their business and that's how they have access, they still have access."

Dick Bell, on the other hand, is not convinced that the nets, especially the Internet itself, is really that much of a Republican stronghold. He says that this is partly because the Democrats and the president are working to broaden the base of the nets. "The president," Bell explains, "has done a lot of work on getting computers distributed into schools and pushing that as a national goal and trying various mechanisms and partnerships as a way of going straight at the fact that people have differential access. You know, if that is the only way that you're going to communicate with people, then you are going to have a problem. In terms of demographics, I don't know. The demographics are pretty soft. On the one hand, if you thought it was only the income distribution, then that might lead you to think that the Republicans would benefit more, but certainly the early [adopters] ... of the Internet [are] not, because [they are] more libertarian than anything else. They have a lot of trouble with the Republicans on the social issues.

"That doesn't mean that they love the Democrats on the economics issues, but it puts them more up for grabs, I think, than anything else. And that's one of the principle reasons that I always felt that we needed to play now, because this is not an audience that was committed one way or the other, and it is people who were consumers of information and were willing to do some weighing and balancing but who appreciated the fact, especially at the beginning, when we first put our Web page up.

"You know, the DNC was the first major party to have a Web site. My site was up for five or six months before the Republicans came on, and in the first month or two, we got a lot of people writing in on the guest books saying, 'We hate you guys, we can't stand what you all are doing, but we really appreciate the fact that you have done this.' And you know, that's one of those funny things about politics on the net—part of it is just being willing, to know what the game is, to have an idea what is going on it this world. People appreciate the fact that you try and that you're reaching out even if they don't necessarily agree with you on the issues."

Some observers believe that the relative youth of the nets and their general relationship with educational institutions will tend to create a constituency that is more favorable to the Democratic Party than to the Republicans. One of those, University of Pennsylvania Professor David Farber, has been active in assisting the Democratic Party and groups related to the Democrats get on the Internet. Professor Farber, who was also one of the small group involved with founding the Internet, says that he thinks liberal groups, including the Democratic Party, are more effective in their use of the Internet, precisely because of the Internet's demographics.

Professor Farber explains: "A lot of people who are on it [the Internet] are college students, who tend to be a little bit more to the liberal side than the conservative side in my experience. Technical people, professionals, tend to be a little bit more in that direction even as they grow up. I think that message gets across the organizations, the groups like EFF [Electronic Frontier Foundation], CDT [Center for Democracy and Technology], and others which are all liberal based are much more visible on the Net. They send out more newsletters. They keep people better informed."

Professor Farber also believes that the more liberal demographics that he sees will lead to liberal institutions making more effective use of the nets. He says that the trend may have started during the 1992 presidential election, but that it took awhile for the nets to reach critical mass. Now that it is happening, Professor Farber expects the trend to continue.

Although there was not much use of the nets during the 1992 campaign, Professor Farber indicated that during the 1996 campaign more people would "try to play there," for two reasons: "One, the community is big enough now so that it serves a reasonable voting pool. You might as well try it and see if you can affect them. The other is, again, back in the organizing. The thing that intrigues me about the Net is that it is composed of people who tend to be topically more active than those who aren't. Tend to be. The pool is dangerous. There also tends, probably, to be a younger constituency, and they tend to have the energy. So, if you can marshal those people, maybe you can actually do something outside."

▶ **Marshaling the Forces**

"Because it [the Internet] makes the transaction cost so cheap, it opens up the possibility of organizing in ways that haven't been opened before," Dick Bell explains, describing how the use of public networks can affect the way political parties handle one of their oldest tasks, communicating with their workers. Where once the major parties were organized in a hierarchical structure that started with block and precinct organizers at the bottom and rose through city, county, and state committees up to the national level, parties now can have communications that reach directly from the national committee to the individual precinct worker. The result is that communications are dramatically speeded up, and the message is more likely to arrive intact.

A number of party workers have also noted that as society changes, getting block- and precinct-level volunteers is becoming more difficult, which in turn means that parties need a different means of communications if they are to continue to function on the local level. Electronic communications can provide a means that is both easy to use and extremely inexpensive, at least from the view of party organizers. It is both easy and cheap because the parties encourage their volunteers to communicate using their own personal computers and electronic-mail accounts. As a result, the volunteer ends up absorbing much of the cost of the communications infrastructure. Because of the growing popularity of personal computers and services, such as CompuServe and America Online, the incremental cost to the volunteers is fairly low, which allows them to communicate with the party at an affordable price, even to the extent of helping provide communications to other volunteers who may not be able to use electronic mail.

Because computers and public network access are not universal, political parties still must resort to at least some of the more traditional methods, including telephone trees and organizational meetings, but these forms of communications can be handled at a lower level and be more distributed. Once they are on line, party volunteers are rewarded with significantly more information than they used to get from their organizations. Both the Republican and Democratic parties, for example, send out electronic newsletters nearly every day, providing the party faithful with everything from pronouncements from officials to ideas about how to hold discussions on topics important to the party.

The manner in which these electronic newsletters are used can vary according to the situation and the officials managing the mailing list. The Democratic Party, for example, used its electronic mailing list heavily during the summer of 1996 to attack the decision by Republican candidate Robert Dole to leave the U.S. Senate. The Republicans, meanwhile, used their e-mail lists to distribute a daily "Scandal List," which detailed the ethical challenges of the White House staff during the final days of the campaign.

Neither party limits these newsletters and other communications to specific volunteers. They are widely available and sent as a matter of course to the media and anyone else who requests them. More targeted communications are also part of the electronic organizing capabilities of public networks. Officials in both parties routinely communicate using e-mail, for example, and both parties also use targeted e-mail mailing lists aimed at specific groups of volunteers.

"I think we use it very well as a communications tool," says Jonathan Knisley, electronics communications coordinator for the Republican National Committee and manager of the day-to-day operations of the Republican Party Internet and on-line service efforts, who also sets up and runs the mailing lists that are used to pass information to volunteers and the press. Knisley said that the Republicans were working on ways of using the Internet to enhance the traditional organizing efforts the party has always used, such as recruiting volunteers. The Democrats were working on a similar effort during the summer of 1996.

According to Knisley, the RNC had learned to collect information from questionnaires that appeared on the Republican Web site and then turn that material and accompanying information over to state and local Republican committees. Both parties collect such information by presenting forms that visitors to their Web sites can fill out if they want to volunteer to work for the party candidates. While the forms are similar to those that visitors fill out to request membership on mailing lists or campaign materials, the parties keep the volunteer lists separate.

Another traditional activity that is still in its formative stages is fund-raising. Because of legal limitations on donations, parties need to make sure that the donors are eligible and that they provide all of the required information. The Democrats accomplished this by providing a form that Web site users could fill in and request donation materials by mail. By the end of the 1996 presidential campaign, the Republican National Committee was experimenting with on-line donations and using credit cards.

▶ **Reaching the Public**

Ultimately, it is neither the campaign workers, volunteers, or the media that elects candidates. It is the public. For this reason, the major parties and the major candidates in 1996 all attempted to attract public interest to their activities on the Internet and the commercial on-line services.

"The primary purpose of the on-line presence has been to communicate the Democratic message to people in the on-line community," explains the DNC's Dick Bell, who ran all aspects of the Democratic efforts on the Internet, was in charge of the Web site for the Democratic National Convention in Chicago and ran the DNC's on-line presence from Washington. "I think the convention has been the peak point," Bell explains, describing how the DNC used audio and video feeds over the Internet to bring the details of the convention to anyone who wanted to see them. There was more. "We had news flashes," Bell said, "we did a lot of Internet chatting."

Bell had a great deal of incentive, because the Democratic National Convention took place just a few days after the Republicans held their convention in San Diego, where, through the efforts of Anne Gavin, the Republican Party instituted the first-ever live events over the Internet of a national political convention.

There were differences, of course. The Republican convention site on the World Wide Web featured interactive audio but relatively few of the on-line "chats" in which participants typed messages to each other, which was the means popular with the Democrats. The Republican conversations were conducted using a cellular phone operated from the convention floor. The result was a significant amount of live and recorded audio from the GOP site, along with a level of interaction similar to that available from the Democrats.

"We looked at how we could get the information about the convention out beyond San Diego to make people feel like they were actually there," explained Gavin, who served as director of communications for the Republican National Convention. Gavin noted that there was a great deal of interest in seeing the full content of the convention by Internet users, at least in part because the national television networks had dramatically reduced coverage to the point where there was relatively little actual coverage of events compared to previous years. In fact, the commercial networks spent much of their coverage with commentary by their own staff, who in turn delivered summaries of all but the key speeches. This limited coverage meant that both political parties felt the need to find a way to provide the full content of the events to people but without the inevitable filtering that took place because of the reduced coverage.

"We wanted to give them [Internet users] the chance to get information about what was happening at the convention, who those people were that were speaking at the convention, what it was that the Republican Party was saying about its nominee, and be able to download almost immediately," explains Gavin. "That was the big goal. Try to get information out directly to people unfiltered. We wanted to make the convention real for people."

According to Gavin, the initial goals of the convention Internet site were aimed at involving the party faithful. "We were looking at it more from a Republican activist point of view," Gavin says, "because they've gotten used to downloading from the Republican National Committee site." Gavin also notes, however, that the convention site was always planned for public consumption from the beginning. "We were always looking for ways to attract voters who tended to fall into the demographics that were favorable to the Republican Party."

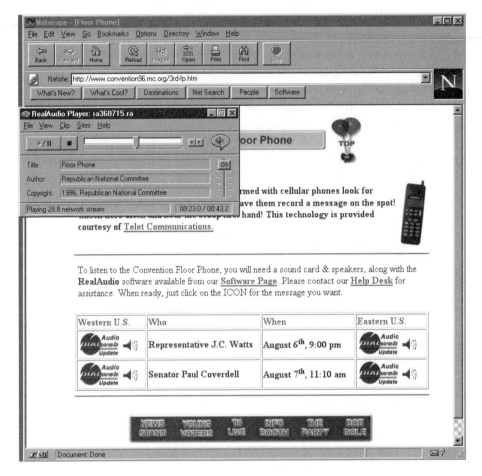

> The Republican National Convention presented for the first time an interactive means of access to the convention floor. Most of the GOP events used audio feeds, including interviews conducted from the floor using a cellular phone, which were then fed directly to the Internet.

One feature that the Republican Party built into its convention was something called the Internet Alley. This was a small space in the upper level of the San Diego Convention Center that Republican organizers assigned to Gavin and her Internet staff. Located nearby were studios operated by the commercial on-line services, CompuServe and American Online. Also nearby was a set of studios operated by nationally broadcast talk shows.

"We wanted to be able to showcase the technology and also provide an area where our speakers and our members of Congress and others could go and almost treat this like any other message delivery system," Gavin explains. "We had a lot of new folks that came in just to have the ability to talk to Newt Gingrich or Colin Powell," says Gavin, explaining how the Internet Alley concept helped build traffic for the convention Web site. "We had over sixty-five news-makers on line, and anybody could talk to them."

▶ Covering the Sites

Both parties found that the news media gravitated toward the increased on-line activity, both because it was something different from the typical political news and because the existence of the convention Internet sites made life easier for members of the media covering the convention. The result was that the Internet operations

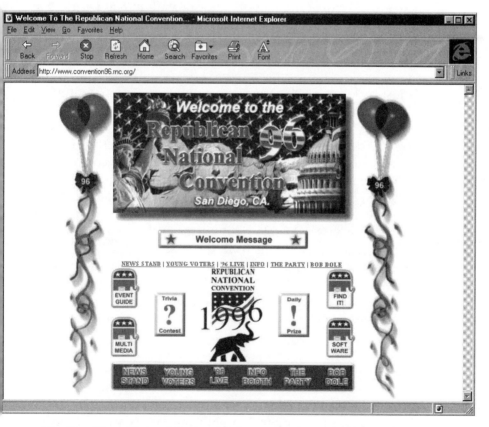

> The Republican National Convention home page featured resources for visitors wanted to learn more bout the party, news and media information, and background on the candidates.

at both conventions were areas of deep media interest, and both parties routinely referred reporters to their Web sites when they requested information.

"We had tons of media there constantly to cover this whole phenomenon of politics on the Internet," Gavin points out. She notes that much of what drew media interest was the tendency for newsmakers to visit the Internet Alley for a few minutes after a stint doing talk radio. Of course, the media also called for more traditional reasons. "Most of them were on-line" Gavin says, "and I referred them specifically to the Web page. We also put the party platform on the Web page." Gavin notes that the media usually preferred getting the information from the convention Web page if they could, rather than walking to the distant media center.

Dick Bell of the Democratic National Committee noticed the same thing. While the Chicago convention facilities did not require the media to take the long hikes they dealt with in San Diego, Bell still noticed that members of the media, in Chicago and elsewhere, were heavy users of the DNC Web site. Part of the reason was that the Democrats were able to get information out on the Internet faster than in almost any other way.

"It just makes it much easier for us to put much more information about things at people's disposal than we otherwise would," Bell explains. "I think the convention has been sort of the peak point for the development of what the party has done thus far. We had a complete, live audio of everything that happened from the podium. We had a live feed that was archived, and then we had a transcribed version of everything that was happening from the podium, so it wasn't speeches as prepared, it was actually the text as delivered that was available right on the Web site with an hour or two lag time from getting it from the basement up to where we were. So, for media who are paying attention to this stuff, and you know more and more of them do, it allows us to service a lot more people in a much shorter span of time at a much lower cost than we could any other way."

▶ Getting the Right Site

Unlike many Web site developers who operate their activities on the nets on a shoestring, both major political parties were relatively well-funded. While the parties looked at the expense of the Internet

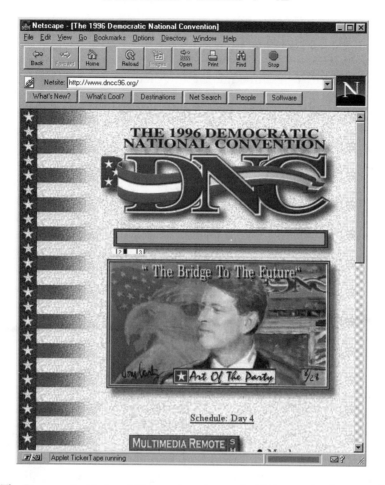

> The Democratic National Convention site on the Web contained many of the same features as the Republican site, but it also had Internet-enabled terminals on the convention floor, which offered direct access between the audience on the Internet and the convention delegates.

activities as fairly minor, when compared to their massive television, radio, and print advertising budgets and their huge media relations staffs, the Internet delivered a lot of bang for the buck, at least according to the people who had to deliver the audience for the parties.

"The major money is going into broadcast media," Bell points out, describing how both parties make the spending decisions that drive their media expenditures. "There are structural reasons for that and also some financial reasons why that is very attractive to people who make the media buys. So, you know, if you look at what all the parties have done so far, I think that you see that no one decided in 1994 that they were really going to put a lot of money and effort into making the Internet a big part of what they were going to do in 1996. However, the same people who made all those decisions would also agree, that it's not going to be like that in four years.

"And it has a lot to do with conservatism. It also has to do with the amount of penetration you have and what is effective to spend money on. Unless you know that you have a lot of people all ready to listen to you in a given medium, television is still a good buy. I think the kind of convergence that's going on and the rate at which people are moving on line, especially if this Internet in a box thing [the Network Computer and Web TV] happens this fall and people really can get on for three or four hundred dollars and a TV set, that will broaden the market out a whole lot. But one way or another, that's going to happen anyway. As it becomes more like a utility and less like something that is very special, I think that you will see a much greater emphasis and much more resources being put into production that goes onto the net."

Much of the money Bell refers to is spent on the computers and network connections that allow the parties to set up shop on the Internet and then provide access to their sites. Much more of it, however, goes to the production costs of creating the Web site, providing material for people to see, and operating the site. The operations alone can require a full-time staffer or two that will update the pages, answer questions, check the things that users say and make sure that requests for information get passed along to the proper people.

"[People] expect an opportunity to interact and not just read what's on the screen, and we tried to keep that in mind," Gavin said, explaining the GOP philosophy for choosing material for the party's convention Web site. "People on the Internet are very demanding. They expect to go to a site and be able to interact with that site, to be able to get things and give things at the same time. We really tried hard to make that work."

Gavin's quest for interactivity led to such things as on-line chat sessions, video and audio conferencing sessions with Republican luminaries, and minute-by-minute updates of the activities at the Republican National Convention. In fact, the Republican Party started its activities a little early. "J. C. Watts [Republican congress-

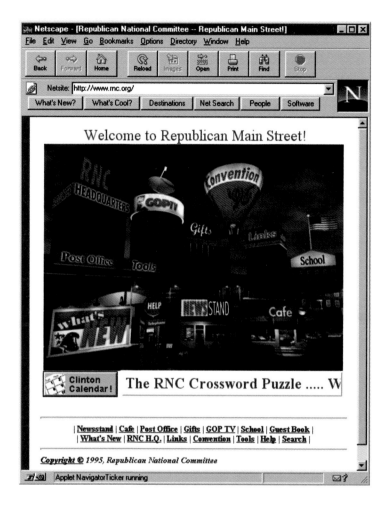

> The Republican National Committee eschewed the standard campaign poster appearance of most political Web sites and chose instead a graphic version of a main street somewhere in the USA. Unlike other Web sites, in which visitors selected from menu items, accessing the RNC site meant selecting one of the pictures. The result was unique, and creative, and it collected a considerable amount of positive press. More important for the Republicans, the site design served to cement the memory of the site for Internet users. There was no doubt that there'd been a visit to the GOP—nothing else looked like it or acted like it.

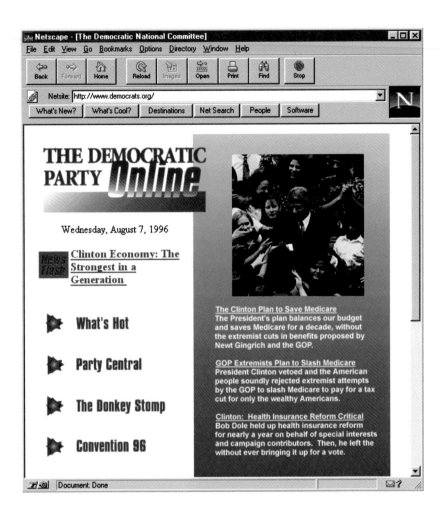

> The Democratic National Committee used a more mainstream approach to the design of their site on the Web. Visitors could navigate using menus, the graphics were mainly campaign photos, and little interactivity was offered. On the other hand, there was plenty of background information, visitors could get the full text of speeches and the like, and there were plenty of links elsewhere.

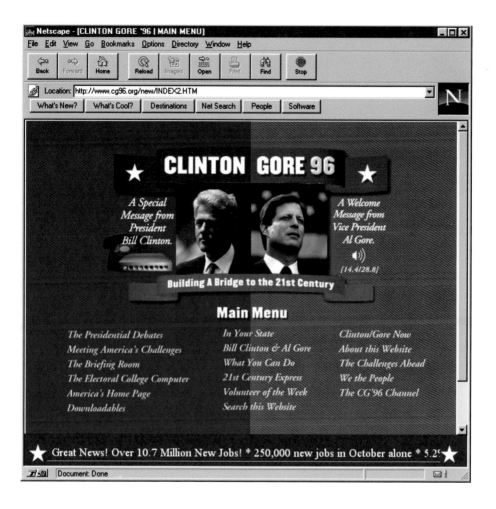

> The Clinton/Gore campaign site was much more dynamic than was the DNC site. The design was more likely to attract the attention of Internet users, and the content changed frequently. In addition, the campaign staff used such multimedia tools as Java applications, audio and video, and animation. The result was a compelling site that received a large number of visitors.

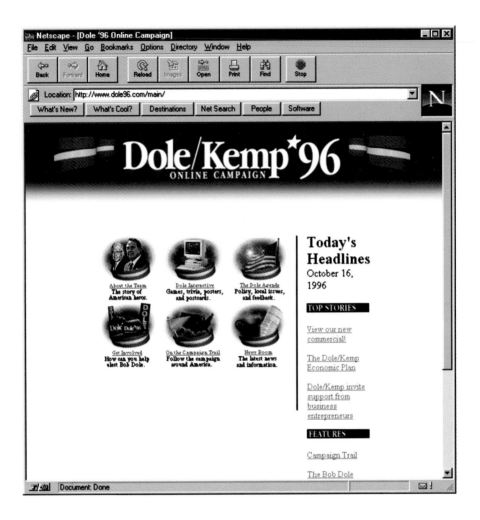

> The Dole/Kemp campaign site was more subdued than the RNC or the Clinton/Gore site. While Dole continued his practice of providing customized information for each repeat visitor, less overall advantage was taken of the medium. The Dole/Kemp site was very thorough in the information it provided for journalists and researchers, but it was less accessible to ordinary voters.

man from Oklahoma] came on Monday night the week before the convention started," Gavin began the story of the first Internet conversation in history from a political convention. "We were just setting up, and we'd told him about it. It was the first time he had ever been on-line." Gavin said that within fifteen minutes Watts had taken over the task of conversing with the on-line audience from the staffers assigned to handle the computer for him, and from the first day was actively looking for ways to interact with the on-line community. "He really loved it," Gavin said.

The Democrats, of course, were watching what the Republicans were doing, and wanted to make sure their party had an impact on their own voters that was at least equivalent. This meant that the Democrats had to move beyond the limits of the Democratic National Committee's Web site, which during the summer of 1996 was mostly a static source of information similar to what appeared in the party's brochures. One of the first tasks was to find a way to present an interactive presence to the Internet community.

"We used the chat facilities, and the area that we were working in was a jointly funded project of all the party committees and the Clinton-Gore Reelect Committee," Bell explained. "So, in a sense, that was our clientele. We concentrated on putting on administration or campaign spokespeople, senators and senatorial candidates, House members and House candidates. We did have a couple of delegates and a state party chair or two. But our primary focus was on people who were running for office at the federal level. We did some work from the floor. The terminals on the floor were Internet enabled. And we did one live chat with Senator [John F.] Kerry from Massachusetts from the floor, and on Thursday night we did a live chat with the Maryland delegation."

▶ Getting Attention

Providing material is only half the battle. For a political party or any other movement to be successful on line, there must also be people who visit the Web page, participate in the forums, or download the speeches and video material. Getting those people is harder than it is with traditional broadcast media, because the material has to be actively sought out. Television, radio, and print ads, by contrast, are delivered to the audience, who passively receives them (or perhaps not so passively changes to another station).

As Anne Gavin mentioned, however, on-line users are demanding. Because most of them are paying for the time they use, they expect the material they access to be useful, interesting, and well-organized. In addition, because many of them are interested in the technology of the Internet, they also expect the Web sites they access to use up-to-the-minute technology where it is appropriate and to use design philosophies that are as interactive as possible.

In fact, users tend to treat Internet sites that simply deliver basic information and are not up to date with considerable derision. One frequently used term for such sites is "brochureware," which clearly describes a collection of information that is not significantly different from what one would find in a company's catalogs or advertising flyers. The Republicans and Democrats, understanding the disdain that goes with the concept of brochureware, did a great deal to avoid being labeled as such. For the most part, they succeeded.

On the other hand, the manner in which the Democrats and Republicans presented themselves, especially in their permanent sites, was quite different. Part of the reason for the differences was that the people responsible for the designs, Jonathan Knisley and Lisa McCormack for the Republicans and Dick Bell for the Democrats, had somewhat different views of their audiences.

As Bell mentioned, the Democratic site was primarily aimed at people who already identified themselves as Democrats. The Republicans, on the other hand, were trying hard to get people who had never had much contact with the Republican Party to take a look. Interestingly, the Democratic site was by far the more conservative of the two.

Of course, just about every party and candidate involved with an issue during the 1996 election had some sort of presence on the Internet that year. Some Web pages were brochureware pure and simple—the graphics on those Web sites looked just like the candidates's campaign material and contained the same information. Other sites went far beyond brochure material and attempted to become centers of information for like-minded visitors.

The two sites with the most funding—the Republican and Democratic national committees—also had the most content and used many of the newest techniques. Cutting-edge technology was not limited to the committees, however, and both major presidential candidates also had extensive sites on the Internet, in some cases using the newest technologies available to bring their stories to people who stopped by on the nets.

"I think looks are important," says Alyson Behr, founder of Behr Communications, a Los Angeles–based company that does Web site design and Internet consulting for a variety of technology and business clients. Behr is also a former magazine editor and has a strong grasp of how the media interact with Web sites. According to Behr, a number of factors will encourage people to investigate a site encountered on the World Wide Web. She feels that the overall appearance of a site and its initial use of technology will get visitors to at least stop and read what is on the home page. But she also feels that there needs to be more if people are going to stay. Behr said that she found the sites of the Republican National Committee and Bob Dole the best of the major parties, although the Democratic National Committee and the Clinton-Gore campaign sites were nearly as good.

"The Republican National Committee," Behr explained, "has really good graphics and really great ideas. Their trivia contest is terrific, and they have really gone out of their way to encourage interactivity with their site." She adds, "Some of the live feeds took forever to download during the convention," noting that the Republican convention site was not without problems. "I thought that in some cases technology got in the way of the interaction with their constituency."

The Dole-Kemp campaign site came up with a unique idea, which Behr thought was well-suited to political use. The idea was a user-specific feature that was able to determine when a user had visited the site earlier and, using that information, was able to deliver a customized home page. Using this feature, a visitor to the Dole-Kemp Web site on the Internet would have the latest information on items they had previously listed as their areas of interest. Thus, the Web site offered visitors the chance to customize the Dole-Kemp home page to suit their interests. Once a user indicated interest in the personalized home page, the site software asked the user several questions designed to determine what they wanted to see. Then, using a new technology pioneered by Netscape, created a "cookie" (a unique identifier provided by the Web site) that identified each user.

In this way, if a user said he was interested in education, defense, and foreign affairs, the Dole Web site would issue the cookie and then keep track of the number it had issued. When that person came back (meaning they were identified by the cookie), the computer supporting the Web site would check for the existence of the cookie and then deliver information on the topics indicated as of interest to the user.

"The Dole idea of the precisely targeted Web site was brilliant," Behr noted, then added that "being able to formulate your own page that lets them know what's important to you and give them the ability to respond was a real stroke of genius."

On the other hand, while Behr liked the overall looks of the Clinton-Gore Web site, she felt that it was not as interactive as it could be, and, more important, she criticized some of the technical issues involving the design of the site. The most significant complaint, according to Behr, was that the Clinton-Gore site had repeated problems delivering its home page images (this was a problem noted by many other observers, including this author). Behr, however, praised the animated slide show developed on the campaign site. "It's interesting that the Clinton-Gore site is very slick and very polished, and it reflects the way Clinton is conducting his campaign," Behr said. "A lot of things are falling into place right now [late October], and his site reflects a very smooth venture."

The sites of other candidates were not up to the same standards as those of the presidential candidates. When Behr reviewed the home page of Republican candidate Patrick Buchanan just before the Republican National Convention, she found it wanting. "Very conservative," she said of the Buchanan presence, "the weakest of all of the sites I've reviewed."

Behr commented that Ross Perot's Reform Party site was better than Buchanan's but still not as good as it could have been. "It was well thought out, and it contained bios and speeches and on-line voting for delegates, and it had multimedia accessories, but there wasn't much opportunity for interaction."

Potentially more important for the long term, the Democratic and Republican national committees use full-time staff members to manage their Web sites and other activities on the nets. This means that the committees have the time and personnel to create a thoroughly designed presence and to manage it on a day-to-day basis. For this reason, Behr spent quite a bit of time studying the Internet sites of the Republicans and Democrats. She thought they were both good, although she thought the Republicans had done a better job. "The Republican site set the standard a couple of months ago [midsummer 1996]," Behr noted. She said she especially like the GOP design in which a graphic representation of a city's downtown was used as a means of navigation through the site. For example, if you wanted to read press releases about Republican candidates, you would click on the newsstand picture.

While Dick Bell derided the Republican design as a representation of an "Amway Nation," the site was extremely popular, and even some Democrats admitted off the record that the Republican site was more effective. Several staffers noted with a mixture of appreciation and confusion the fact that the Republican National Committee Web site includes a link to the Democratic National Committee—a favor the Democrats have not returned.

One of the most effective features of the Republican site for Internet users was its interactivity. As was the case with many political sites on the nets, you could download sound and video files, and you could fill out forms volunteering to help out the party, but the Republicans had quite a bit more. One popular item was the site's guest book. Normally an Internet site guest book is a form that visitors to the site fill out with their comments and is then read by the Webmaster as a way to glean suggestions or find out what users might want to see. The Republicans went a step further, however, and made their guest book public. Anyone could read through the thousands of entries and see what other visitors liked and did not like about the Republican National Committee's Web site.

According to Jonathan Knisley, the guest book was an important feature, both because other users seemed to like reading the comments and because the GOP staff made it a point to implement suggestions where possible. Knisley said that when a suggestion was made in the site's early days to publish e-mail addresses and phone numbers, that information was added the next day. That allowed visitors to the Republican site to send e-mail to any Republican staffer, from Chairman Haley Barbour on down, with a single click of the mouse button.

Knisley also decided to create a series of discussion groups, much like the forums that populate on-line services, so that visitors could carry on continuing discussions about the party and its activities. With the exception of four or five messages that contained highly offensive language, the Republicans made no effort to censor any of the material posted by users. According to Knisley, the only way to be taken seriously by users on the Internet was to be willing to listen to them, whether or not they agreed with the Republican Party.

The Democratic National Committee was on line well before the Republicans. In fact, the beginnings of the DNC effort stemmed

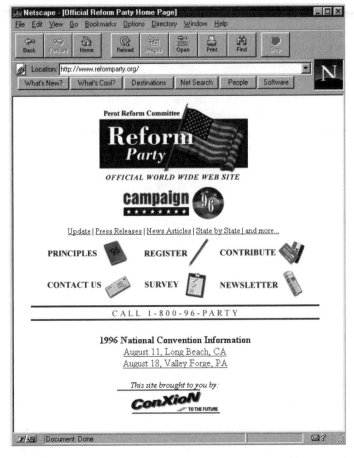

> Party activity on the Internet was not limited to the Republicans and Democrats. The Reform Party was also active and, in fact, conducted portions of its convention on line.

from earlier efforts during the 1992 presidential campaign, during which Jock Gill used e-mail and discussion groups on America Online and CompuServe to spread the word about Bill Clinton. When the first DNC Web site first went live, it was also the first time any major political party had done anything like that. As a result, the Democrats went with what they had seen elsewhere on the Web, and, initially, it was a good effort, but certainly not a great effort.

It did not take long, however, for the Democrats to learn more about what users of the nets wanted and to make changes. The party revised some material, added new items, and made the site more interesting. Eventually, users were able to enjoy animation, video, and sound, and they could see clips of speeches or read

Democratic issue papers. Unlike the Republican site, however, the DNC did not offer any real interaction for Internet users. While the DNC did create a guest book, it was not open to everyone and there were no discussion groups or chat rooms. Despite the limitations, the Democratic site was well-received by users of the Internet. According to Dick Bell, the general response was that visitors appreciated the DNC's efforts to bring their position on line.

Behr thought the Democrats could have done more. She noted that most of the interaction was in the form of asking for information, but there was little two-way flow. She also noted that the DNC did not have e-mail addresses available and that you could not even find the phone number for DNC headquarters. "Basically, it's fairly minimal," Behr said. "They did have a sort of a muckraking area called the Donkey Stomp, but I noticed several typographical errors, grammatical errors and some poor [HTML] coding."

One interesting fact revealed by both parties was the unexpected interest from visitors outside the United States. Staffers from both parties noted that visitors from overseas expressed interest in joining the parties, in making contributions, and in learning more about American politics. Knisley noted that membership requests came from throughout the world—as far away as Israel and South Africa.

While the national parties have the most money to spend and the greatest amount of information to distribute, and for that reason the most elaborate on-line sites, many state committees and statewide candidates worked hard to create a presence on the nets. The most widely used of such sites were in states that have a relatively large number of Internet users and a deep penetration of technology industries, such as California, Oregon and Massachusetts. A number of observers said that the 1995 special election in Oregon for the U.S. Senate was the first election in which the Internet made the difference. In 1996 it may have been the Senate race in Massachusetts, in which the influence of the on-line communities and the information that traveled through the nets made enough difference to affect the election.

▶ The Massachusetts Senate Election and the Kerry Plan

The battle for the Massachusetts seat in the U.S. Senate in 1996 had all the marks of a close, intense race. It was a race between two popular politicians, the incumbent Democratic Senator John Kerry and the highly regarded Republican Governor William Weld. Both men had recently won statewide elections, both had similar moderate views, and both had broad popular support for their candidacies and their views. There were differences, of course. For example, Kerry was more popular with the environmental movement, and Weld was more popular with fiscal conservatives. The two candidates resembled each other in their view that the campaign should be run in a manner that spared voters from personal attacks and negative campaigning.

There was also another difference. Kerry created an Internet campaign office and started working on an on-line presence nearly six months before the election, while Weld only managed to go on line with a minimally functional site on the Internet five or six weeks before the election. Kerry used his on-line capability for everything from recruiting volunteers to populating rallies, while Weld rarely used his site. In the end, Kerry beat Weld by about six percentage points.

Was this win a result of Kerry's heavy Internet focus? Did the nets contribute to a Kerry win? It is impossible to know for sure, but there are clear indications that Kerry's activities on the Internet and commercial on-line services helped build his percentages and probably helped cement his position in the large high-technology communities in Massachusetts. Unfortunately, because the means to measure conclusively the impact of the nets on the election do not yet exist, the evidence can be presented, but proof still escapes us.

When the Kerry campaign staff began planning its Internet presence in February 1996, one of the first actions the staff took was to hire an experienced professional, Dr. Eric Loeb, to handle the design and implementation of the Web site. Dr. Loeb had implemented a similar site in 1994 for the reelection effort of Massachusetts Senator Ted Kennedy, creating what the Democrats claim was the first campaign Web site anywhere. In charge of the effort for the campaign staff was senior Kerry campaign staffer Ben Green, who was responsible for a number of tasks in the campaign, including opposition research. He was also responsible for making material available on the Kerry Web site, including position papers, press releases, schedules, and so forth.

Initially, the idea behind the Kerry Internet presence was involvement. "The most important thing is that it be a resource for political participation," Loeb explained. "The thing that concerns me most is that you have a process for bringing people in, for incorporating people, and making sure that political interest actually turns into political involvement." Dr. Loeb also noted that having a well-designed Web page was critical to the process of involvement and stressed that the Web site and Internet presence could not exist successfully without also having campaign staff that could back it up. Loeb said that if he had the funds, he would like to add a research staff person to specifically handle interaction through the Internet. "There is this idea of the Internet being a community-based medium," Loeb said, explaining why he felt that such a presence would help the campaign in Massachusetts. "I'd like to see that come to fruition here in this campaign. I'd like to see excitement about what we can do ourselves and for our community using the Internet."

Loeb had the Kerry Internet site running about a month after he got the initial approval. At first, the site was fairly limited. According to Loeb, it was mainly the same sort of material that someone could pick up at a campaign office. In addition, drawing on the experience in the Kennedy campaign and from the lessons of the 1992 Clinton Internet staff, Loeb also included features that allowed visitors to the Kerry site to sign up as volunteers, offer to donate money, and request information.

Once the site was running, the Kerry Internet staff began to enjoy the benefits of even the basic capabilities. For example, according to Ben Green, more than a thousand people signed up as volunteers through the forms available on the Internet. Green also said that the campaign staff used the Internet facilities to recruit media monitors—people who watched for items about Senator Kerry in papers outside of Boston. "These would be people in the outlying areas, in the outmarket newspapers, and the smaller market televisions stations," Green said. The media monitors then sent in their reports through the Internet and faxed clippings of stories to the media staff at the Kerry headquarters in Boston. Green said that without the media monitors spread throughout the state keeping up with what was actually being said about their candidate would have been extremely difficult.

"We had about seventy-five people statewide who were helping us with this," Green said, then noted that they had additional roles as well. "These people would get into political chat rooms [an interactive discussion on the Internet, CompuServe, or America Online where people type their conversations to each other], and they would talk up John Kerry based on the information that was on our

Web site, and they would report back to me on what exactly was taking place in these chat rooms."

Green said that one of the most popular areas on the Internet for discussions of the Senatorial race was on the Web Site belonging to the *Boston Globe* (http://www.boston.com), which ran a number of political chat rooms. Green also said that the Kerry staff noticed that there was a considerable "spike" in user interest in both their Web site and in the activity in the chat rooms immediately after each of the nine debates conducted by the candidates, and he made it a point to have staff on hand to engage in these chats.

"Basically our strategy was to get people involved, people that otherwise would not be involved," Green says, explaining another important objective of the Internet office, "and in that regard, it was a tremendous success in getting people involved and in reaching out to every corner of the state. I don't think there's any other medium by which this can be accomplished."

Of course, some of the efforts of the Kerry Internet staff were aimed more at traditional organizing efforts, such as encouraging the Kerry faithful to appear at rallies, write letters, or go to the polls and vote. To accomplish this, Green and the Kerry volunteer coordinators set up a carefully designed set of electronic mailing lists that included everyone from key supporters, party operatives, and even college students.

"We had one group we called 'Team Kerry,'" Green said. "These were people who had filled out volunteer forms on the page, or who had included their e-mail address on volunteer sign-up sheets." Green said that by the end of the campaign, Team Kerry and others included more than three thousand e-mail addresses. Because virtually every college student has an e-mail address, the Kerry staff included college Democrats on their e-mail lists and then created a subgroup of college Democratic leaders.

"We could pull things together at the last minute by putting out an e-mail," Green said, describing one way that the campaign capitalized on the immediacy of electronic mail. "It's a lot easier than making phone calls, because with the click of a mouse I can get a message out to three thousand people. The volunteer coordinator would write something up, forward it to me, and I would forward it on out to our volunteers," Green explained, "and it proved to be effective."

One instance in particular played a critical role in the campaign. It happened when the campaign momentum stalled following a se-

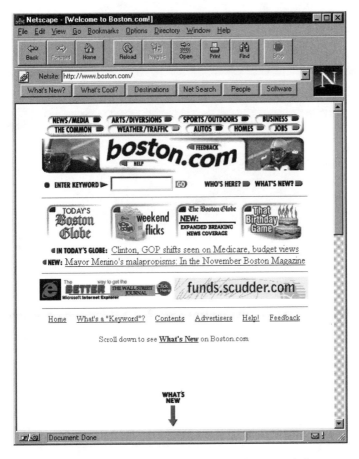

> Demonstrating that all politics is local, the Web page of the *Boston Globe* (www.Boston.com) was at least partly responsible for the intense Internet interest in Massachusetts politics. This site was also pivotal in the success of Democratic Senator John Kerry's Internet activities.

ries of attacks by Weld that questioned Kerry's ethics during his divorce several years earlier. "There was a point toward the end of October where the *Globe* was running a series of critical stories on Senator Kerry, and Governor Wells was raising a series of questions on the senator's ethics," Green said. "The Weld campaign picked up on this story. This blunted our momentum."

"The story came out on a Friday. On Saturday morning Weld called a press conference, asking for a Senate Ethics Committee investigation. We had a big rally planned for that day, and we absolutely needed a big turnout for that rally. So, on Friday evening I

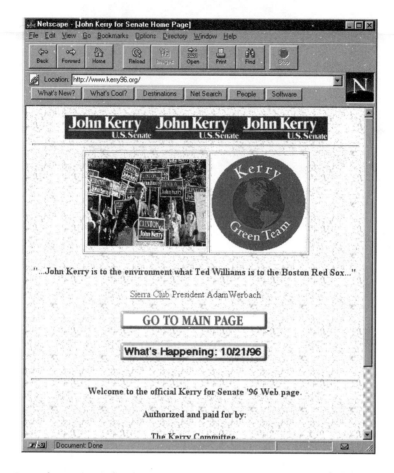

> Incumbent Massachusetts Senator John Kerry was extremely active on the Internet during the 1996 campaign. This activity may have played a crucial role in the success of his reelection bid.

blasted out an e-mail to people to please come to the rally to support Senator Kerry. We got a great turnout—we got over two hundred fifty people that showed up. I would say that over a third of those people had found out about it from the e-mail."

"It was a critical moment," Green concluded. "It was critical that we had a large crowd at this event, both to show the appearance to the press that we were on track and for Senator Kerry's confidence, and to show him that we were going to ride this thing out and move on."

Green adds that while the Internet site did not play such a critical role every day, it did a lot to create the perception that the Kerry campaign as a group had its act together and that it was leaving no stone unturned in reaching out to the people of Massachusetts. "It absolutely made a difference," Green said.

▶ Bypassing the Media

One of the factors that played a significant role in the choice of material for the Kerry Web site echoed the choices made by other campaigns at all levels and in each area. That factor was a perceived need on the part of campaign organizers to avoid the interpretations of the news media. In the case of the Kerry campaign, in fact, there were really two sorts of efforts with regard to the press—an attempt to make sure that the media got the information that the campaign wanted to get out that way and an attempt to make sure that the information for voters got out without a filter.

Green says that on one hand the Kerry campaign sent out a number of press releases that were aimed at providing background information to the media, while others were more useful to the average voter. He adds that the Kerry campaign tried to keep the tone of the material posted to their Internet site positive and as useful as possible to as many people as possible.

In fact, the desire to get information to voters without a filter may be one of the persistent themes of political use of the nets. While the organizational power of the nets may be one of the items that most influenced the vote in 1996, it is the effort to avoid the seven-second sound bite and the quick quote that is most influencing the willingness to spend money and allocate resources to on-line sites.

Interestingly, much of the effort of the national media, especially the television networks, tends to encourage such efforts. The coverage of the 1996 party conventions was abbreviated much more than in previous years, while at the same time, much of the coverage was devoted to summaries and analysis by pundits rather than simply broadcasting the events themselves. Adding to the problem, at least from the point of view of the party committees, is the fact that newspaper reportage is dying out in all but a few cities. While *The Washington Post, The New York Times,* and a few other large newspapers devote enough space so that their coverage is essentially total, other papers, such as *USA Today,* report on politics in a much more limited fashion.

The shortage of coverage is compounded by the fact that most candidates and parties, regardless of where they may fall on the political spectrum, seem to feel that the news media are not reporting

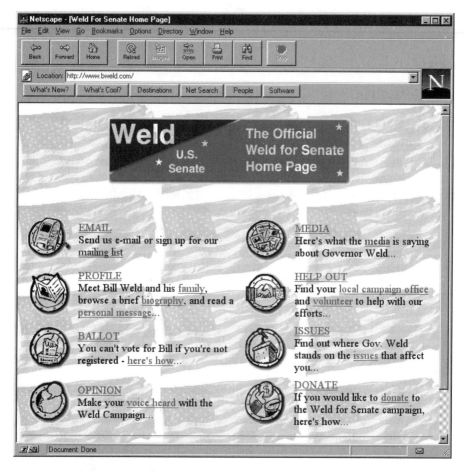

> Republican Governor William Weld, who was challenging Senator John Kerry for the U.S. Senate, did not get a site on the Internet until the campaign was nearly over, and even that site was never completed.

their take on the issues with sufficient depth or accuracy. This persistent complaint, heard in virtually every interview, plays a large role in helping these organizations decide to create sites on the Internet, assign staff to keep them updated, and make sure that questions are answered. In every case, just as the Kerry campaign assigned media monitors to feed the party line in chat sessions, the candidate's organizations most want to be in charge of the content of the message. By having a Web site where anyone with Internet access can download the full text of whatever they want to read, the candidates and parties can do this.

▶ Yours In Trendiness

In 1996, just because the campaigns and committees wanted to get their messages out in their own way, that did not mean they did not want press coverage. In fact, they wanted as much coverage as they could get, regardless of the medium or the outlet. Again, the campaign Web sites came into play.

During the 1996 election, one favorite topic of media everywhere was the Internet, to the point that it could fairly be called a fad (or even a craze). Newspapers as staid as the *The New York Times* were devoting dozens of pages every week to reporting on the Internet. Features in general-circulation newspapers and magazines were listing Web site URLs (uniform resource locators). Internet addresses were turning up on everything from beer ads to campaign literature. The Internet was hot.

Combining the Internet's trendiness with the presidential elections in 1996 was a natural. No outlet appears to have missed any opportunity to write about it frequently, which meant that publications as diverse as *PC Magazine* and the *The Washington Post* ran features covering politics on the Internet. Likewise, the television networks featured Internet stories frequently. This was boosted during July 1996 with the launch of MSNBC, the cable television and Internet news outlet created jointly by Microsoft and NBC. This organization, which featured heavy political coverage, meant that NBC had a larger than usual share of Internet-related political stories on its hands, and it made use of them. *NBC Nightly News* frequently included stories of politics on the Internet, as did NBC-owned and affiliated stations.

This general trend encouraged newspaper and broadcast outlets to feature political Internet stories where there was something significant to report. In the case of the Massachusetts Senate race, there was usually broad favorable coverage of the Kerry Web site and little coverage of Weld, because the governor did not even have a presence on the Internet until after Labor Day, by which time most of the broadcast outlets were covering serious campaign issues rather than the features they ran during the summer.

Although news coverage of the Internet activities by a political campaign was unlikely to make a critical difference in the outcome of an election, it did help create a generally favorable response, at least among voters who were aware of the Internet and who wanted to feel that the candidates in which they had an interest were up to date with technology. Early in the primary season, for example, the Dole campaign received a great deal of press for its strong site (at least compared with the rest of the field). Later, when candidate Dole gave out his Web site's URL at the end of the first presidential debate, many Internet users expressed appreciation for his doing so.

More important, Dole received more coverage for giving out the address and then even more when a Democratic sympathizer put up a bogus Web site with a nearly identical name. All of this interest would not have come to the Dole campaign had the candidate not said something, and the coverage was in general favorable to Dole.

As Chapter 7, "The Press and Politics in Cyberspace," points out, there are a number of ways that a candidate or a movement can get sympathetic or even positive coverage, and, in many cases, it only requires that the press get their hands on useful material. Much of the business of the politicians and their staffs with regard to the nets in 1996 was to make sure that the material was there and that the press and the voters could find it.

▶ But Does It Win Elections?

The fact is, with few exceptions, campaign staffs do not know for sure what wins elections. The best they can do is to try whatever worked during the last election and hope that it works again. The problem is that there are few definitive measures in politics, and few people who can interpret what few measures do exist. This means that not only do political staffs not know for sure whether the work they do on the Internet or the commercial on-line services gains voters, they do not necessarily know whether a specific television commercial will work or whether the phrasing of a specific speech will strike a chord with the voters. Similarly, when a campaign launches a new ad on television and the numbers in the polls immediately drop, it could, of course, be that the voters do not like the ad, but it could also be that some other event, independent of the ads, led to the drop.

For most campaigns and in most elections it is difficult to identify what makes a difference and what does not. Still, there are instances in which it is possible to be reasonably certain that a particular event, such as a critical rally or a specific television spot, made a difference. A campaign that can use the lessons from that event can sometimes make a big difference, which is why the lesson of the e-mail drive to turn out people for the Kerry rally in October provides an important lesson. It was clear in that case that a big turnout was important to jump start the campaign's momentum and that using the Internet to deliver a last-minute appeal worked. No other means could have delivered the word to the necessary number of supporters in time.

Such definitive events do not happen all that often in a campaign, however, which means that to learn for sure what the impact might have been, some group with pockets deep enough to fund the necessary polls and focus groups and fund the required analysis will have to study what the nets really did to the political process during the election of 1996. In the meantime, we have considerable anecdotal evidence, and we have some stories in which it seems clear that specific events during the campaign were affected.

In fact, in many cases the effect on events was quite clear, as was the case in the Kerry rally in October. Ben Green was able to tell that about a third of the attendees were there because they received the e-mailed plea to attend. Likewise, Green was able to provide information on press coverage and even chat room trends statewide through his network of media monitors that communicated with him across the Internet. Each of those events, each trend, and each news story played some incremental role in bringing the majority of the vote to John Kerry.

On the other hand, none of these events in itself made a difference to the outcome of the election. The same could be said for nearly any other event in nearly any other race—most of the time, there is simply no single event so crucial that it affects the outcome—but there are exceptions.

For example, during the 1996 Senate election in Virginia, Republican John Warner found that one of his media consultants had electronically altered a photo of his opponent, Mark Warner, to appear that Democrat Warner was shaking hands with Bill Clinton at a rally. In fact, Mark Warner had not been photographed in such a pose and was quick to produce the unaltered news photo as proof. Had John Warner not been about twenty points ahead in the polls when that happened, this single event could have cost him a critical part of his margin and, perhaps in so doing, the election. As it was, it gave Democrat Mark Warner a much needed hook with which to challenge the ethics of Republican John Warner. When the votes were counted, the margin had shrunk to only 6 percent.

In the Virginia race, the single event was a poorly chosen advertisement. It could just as easily have been on a candidate's Web site or in an e-mail message to the press. There are times, as this event shows, in which a single event can have a significant effect on the outcome of an election. Even experienced campaign staffers rarely know ahead of time what those events will be (if he had, John Warner's media consultant certainly would not have run that ad). It is possible only after the fact to determine what worked.

Just as we know that faking evidence can lead to big trouble for a candidate, we are beginning to find out that a well-designed and well-considered presence on the Internet and the commercial services can play an important role in traditional politics. In some cases, as was the case in John Kerry's campaign in Massachusetts, it may make a critical difference.

What we do know is that taking politics to the nets can result in several specific things that most campaigns and most candidates want.

- **Unfiltered access to the voters.** Many campaigns and most candidates find this to be the most compelling reason of all to take to the nets. Their word gets out as they intended, without the interpretation of the media. The voters get the full product of the candidate's staff in just the way the candidate wants it.

- **Fast and inexpensive access to workers.** The nets are first and foremost a communications medium and that means that campaigns have a way to get important messages to their volunteers instantly and without fear of the message being lost, changed, garbled, or delayed. This also has the benefit of requiring far fewer intermediaries, which means that more volunteers can be in contact with voters, and fewer need to do administrative tasks.

- **Effective access to the media.** While candidates and parties do not want their message filtered, they still want coverage. The media, suffering downsizing along with the rest of business, make heavy use of computer-assisted reporting as a way to make up for staff shortages. A presence on the nets provides a highly effective means of getting a candidate's message to the media quickly and inexpensively.

- **Control over perceptions.** The means that how a candidate is presented on his Internet site can have an important effect on the underlying perceptions of voters. While it is by no means the only perception (otherwise Bob Dole would have won), it does contribute to the overall perception that the technically aware voter has of the candidate, and this can translate into a more sympathetic reception for the candidate's messages.

• **Feedback from voters.** One characteristic of the nets that has not been matched by broadcast and print media is that the nets are interactive. A candidate or a political party can learn what interests voters, how they feel about the positions taken, and how the issues affect the voters. Used properly and communicated with campaign planners, this feature has the potential for fine-tuning a campaign in ways that no other medium can provide. While little use has been made of this capability, campaign staffers are beginning to realize the potential power and are discussing ways to use the interactivity of the nets next time.

While traditional politics is still learning how to use the new media of the nets effectively, the indications are clear that the lessons are already starting to take hold. The staffs at political parties are making their on-line operations a permanent part of their planning, and fewer politicians would consider running a statewide or national campaign that did not include active use of the nets. Still, there are successful candidates that have no presence on line, just as there are successful candidates who rarely advertise on television. Clearly, in smaller districts where physical contact with the candidate is more crucial, electronic media are less important. On the other hand, in 1996 many congressional races were active on line, and there were quite a few state legislature races that used the nets.

It is equally clear that this trend, now started, will continue. As was the case with television in the election of 1960, we now realize that the new medium of electronic communications is important. We now need to learn just how important it is and in what way this new medium can be used. Those lessons are still in the future but probably not very far off. You can be assured that the 1998 Senate and House races will see much heavier use of the new medium. By the presidential election of 2000 the new medium will be ubiquitous.

View Go Bookmarks Options Directory Window Help

Home   Reload   Open   Print   Find   Stop

http://www.democrats.org/

What's New?   What's Cool?   Destinations   Net Search   People   Software

Nontraditional
Politics

"As it happened, I had an account on the old ARPANET," Jerry Pournelle explains, telling the story of what may have been one of the first recorded instances in which the nets played a role in changing legislation. Around 1980, Pournelle, now a well-known science fiction author and computer magazine columnist, was involved in some of the research that eventually led to the Global Positioning System (GPS). Pournelle says that he went to the net (in those days, it was the precursor to the Internet called ARPANET, which was run by the Department of Defense Advanced Research Projects Agency) to tell others what happened.

"I got a phone call from Colonel [Francis X.] Kane [former director of plans, U.S. Air Force System Command], who was the guy who invented the system," Pournelle explains. "Congress had actually zeroed these things out. They [the GPS satellites] were not going to be built, if you can imagine something as useful as that not being built. I sent a message to a couple of guys at [Lawrence] Livermore [National Laboratories], and a couple of Ed Teller's people thought this was a very dumb move on the part of Congress." Pournelle then provided certain officials with information that they used to persuade a few key members of congress not to kill GPS. He says that because of this pressure the program survived and today is rapidly becoming a critical new technology that helps everything from air travel to surveying. "All of that was basically as a result of the existence of the ARPANET," Pournelle says. "We wouldn't have had that system if it wasn't for that."

Nearly fifteen years later, Pournelle once again found himself in the process of planning political action on line, this time in the interest of low-cost space travel. "The DC-X single-stage-to-orbit [SSTO] spaceship was accomplished through a series of meetings of some private adviser groups," Pournelle says. While this sounds ordinary enough, Pournelle goes on to explain that all but the first of these meetings were held on line. "We couldn't have done most of that without a network information utility," Pournelle says, describing an informal group of scientists, engineers, and space advocates that worked together on line for years, quietly putting the plans together and then shepherding them through the process of getting the plans approved, the money allocated, and an actual flying version of their spaceship built and launched.

"We used the old BIX system," Pournelle says, "and it's very primitive compared to what's being done with the Internet these days. We didn't do any real time conversations or video, but I don't think we could have got the papers written or the stuff coordinated without it."

"The Congressional staff [were] on the East Coast, and [the researchers were] out here on the West Coast, and the time zones are different," Pournelle says, explaining how the problems of location affected his effort, "Some of the people [were] involved in doing other things, and everybody had to work on this stuff when they had time."

Pournelle relates one of the classic problems that face organizations that must conduct business across time zones. In his case, the business he was conducting was being done by a loose collection of people sharing a common interest in seeing low-cost access to space succeed. Compounding the problem of time zones and distance, the people involved in planning and promoting the concept all had lives and jobs outside of the SSTO project, which meant that they could work on position papers and attend briefings or discuss design issues only during their spare time. Since one person's spare time rarely coincided with that of anyone else, they needed a means of communication that was free from the constraints of both time and space.

As it happened, Pournelle was a major participant in BIX, a new on-line service being developed by *Byte Magazine* in the mid-1980s. Pournelle was able to persuade the managers of BIX to create a set of space-related conferences (as the forums on that service are called), some of which he used as a home base for his work on the SSTO project. Because BIX offers both private conferences and Internet e-mail, Pournelle was able to conduct on-line meetings and planning sessions, while using his access to the Internet as a way to communicate with officials involved with government space funding and with congressional staffers who had their hands on the legislation.

Pournelle's project began when he and his colleagues decided to present their project to then Vice President Dan Quayle, who chaired the National Space Council during the George Bush administration. Neither Pournelle nor his colleagues had the time to travel to a place where they could assemble the facts for the proposal that a single-stage-to-orbit rocket was technically feasible and that it would save money, specifically by requiring only thirty-five people for a launch (versus twenty thousand for a space shuttle launch), be reusable (the shuttle discards most of the spacecraft), and use newer technology. Instead, Pournelle and his team began developing the presentation and the supporting documentation using BIX as an on-line conferencing system. The service supported their need to share documents, discussions, and plans, and, as a result, the group was able to meet with Quayle in 1989. The presentation was a success, and Quayle endorsed the concept.

Of course, that was only part of the battle. Once they had support from the White House, Pournelle and his team had to gather support from the military, NASA, and Congress. During the next four years, the project went from just a concept and preliminary design to one supported by the U.S. Air Force and NASA and eventually became a flying prototype built by McDonnell-Douglas.

At each stage, the project faced cancellation, funding cuts, and efforts to siphon personnel and support to other projects. At each step, an informal network of backers—congressional staffers, people working on the programs, and interested observers—alerted the team to pending changes, efforts to make changes the group did not support, and to sudden requirements to explain or justify the project. Likewise, the group was able to intervene in a number or last-minute changes in legislation that would have terminated the project.

Eventually, after the first successful flights, the DC-X prototype rocket faced one last attempt to bring it to an end—the sudden removal of money from the U.S. Air Force budget to pay for the fuel for its last series of test flights. There, too, the on-line connections worked. When the group found that it would be impossible to recover the missing funding, they generated a proposal almost overnight that NASA pick up responsibility for the project, then a presentation that Pournelle delivered to the NASA administrator, Dan Goldin, a few days later. Once again, it was a message from a congressional staffer, this time Timothy B. Kyger, that alerted the group to the need for immediate action. They produced the necessary briefings and documentation, gathered support, and made the presentation. They succeeded, and the craft was able to continue its flight testing.

Meanwhile, Pournelle had been meeting with members of Congress about the capability to deliver information so quickly. One of those he met was Georgia Republican Newt Gingrich, who saw for himself how conferencing worked when Pournelle demonstrated BIX during a brief visit to Atlanta. Later, when Gingrich became speaker of the House, he continued to support Pournelle's efforts and became a supporter of the Internet as a way to provide information publicly.

Pournelle's group continues to exist. It is still an ad hoc gathering of engineers, scientists, and space advocates, but now the group is working with other organizations, including the Space Transportation Association and the Space Access Society, among others, to continue the quest for low-cost access to space.

▶ Effectiveness On Line

Unlike many groups that tried to produce a political result early on, the ad hoc space advocacy group established through the efforts of Jerry Pournelle and others produced results. The fact that it was able to influence both legislation and the bureaucracy was due partly to the fact that the participants had a keen understanding of how political pressure works in Washington. In addition, the participants had a solid understanding of how on-line services work, their strengths and weaknesses, and, perhaps more important, what their strengths are not. As a result, the group used an on-line service effectively for communications, planning, and time and space independence but made no attempt to send e-mail messages to legislators unprepared for the reception of e-mail.

The specifics of how the benefits of an on-line service fit into their communication needs makes Pournelle's group an important example. Because the people involved already shared a common objective, and because they were not involved with organizational issues, this informal group was able to focus its attention on its goal, unencumbered by the necessity of running meetings, electing officers, or providing member services. Here's a look at the details:

- **Understanding the medium.** The members of Pournelle's ad hoc group had been using on-line services or the Internet for years. They already knew how to post messages, create e-mail, and place documents on-line for others to share. This meant that the technical issues of handling the logistics and training for an on-line organization could mostly be bypassed, once the participants agreed to use a specific service or agreed to deal with the process through Internet-based e-mail.

- **Understanding the process.** The group quickly began conducting discussions using e-mail, adding comments to position papers electronically and making sure that everyone involved was kept informed. That way, individual members of the group could work on their areas of expertise without impacting on the other members. It also meant that the group members could take submitted information from others and assemble it into a final document that could be used in a formal presentation or proposal.

- **Maximizing resources.** Not everyone who helped needed to be part of the working group. Because Pournelle's group was using an on-line service connected to the Internet, they could receive information from government sources that might not be allowed to participate in the planning or advocacy. Thus, for example, a sympathetic government employee could alert the group that the DC-X budget was under attack by a contractor that was threatened by the prospect of a new type of space access. This would give the group time to prepare a response before any action took place.

- **Knowing the limits.** Despite the fact that the group was quite effective in their informal, net-based organization, they knew that not everyone in the government felt the same way. For that reason, the group did not attempt to use e-mail communications with members of Congress or the Bush administration. Instead, the on-line service was used where it was most effective.

- **Using the medium as leverage.** Instead of being hampered by time zone differences, Pournelle's group used them to its advantage. Because most events affecting the space program happened before 5:00 P.M. Eastern Standard Time, the group's West Coast members still had nearly half a day in which to work and could be warned of an impending problem at the close of business in Washington, D.C., start working on a response almost immediately, and frequently have a response, point paper, or presentation ready by the next morning. Effectively, the group was able to turn around material almost instantly, at least from the point of view in Washington.

- **A reliance on interactivity.** Where the group differs most from the commonly held views of the Internet is that it has never created a home page, never built a Web site, and never become part of what MIT researcher Mark Bonchek calls the "broadcast" media. Instead, the group used the interactivity of the nets to produce work and skipped any effort to create billboards or brochures.

This appreciation of the best ways to use the nets effectively led to a measurable amount of success for the SSTO backers. It also showed dramatically that a group that cannot exist anywhere except on the nets can create effective work in ways that would also be impossible without the nets. Most interesting of all, the government officials on the receiving end of all of this net-based information never realized that they were in the beginning of a vast political experiment. They just thought that the space advocates were unusually well-prepared.

▶ All Politics Is Local

During the spring 1996 battle surrounding a proposed new baseball stadium near Washington, D.C., one county executive lamented the growing technical sophistication of local groups opposing development in northern Virginia, thereby opposing the stadium. He said that it was now possible to create the impression of a huge movement by simply leveraging the ability to use e-mail. Local groups such as the ones opposing development near Washington are developing Web sites, producing list servers, and communicating with their members and with other groups by e-mail across the nets. While such techniques are giving local officials fits, they are not all new. Instead, governments are just now realizing the power that such political groups have when they use the tools of communications available on the Internet and elsewhere.

In March 1993, Internet activist Jim Warren made waves by suggesting that the California legislature make its legislative information, including pending bills, available over the Internet. Warren, who is known to students of the Internet for his long-running mailing list on government access, government intrusion, and privacy issues, was responding to a copy of a bill he had received from California Assemblywoman Debra Bowen that proposed that such information already computerized be made available to anyone in the state. Warren entered the picture by writing a column in a computer magazine in support of the effort. When he was subsequently informed by Bowen's office that the bill probably would not pass because of a lack of support, Warren got busy.

"I went on the net that evening and I already had hundreds of e-mail addresses of people who knew me that I had interacted with on various previous endeavors, and I just broadcast a message across the net saying, 'Hey, this is happening and we ought to support it.'" Warren says that the next step was to help the legislature determine that getting the information on the Internet was both easy and inexpensive, but it turned out that the problems were only starting. What Warren had not realized was that the legislative information Bowen wanted to make available was already being sold for thousands of dollars, that is, such public information as the text of laws and regulations by the state of California to private contractors, lawyers, lobbyists, and so on, generating a huge off-budget revenue stream for the state government. That, and the fact that a number of legislatures resented Bowen's attempt to change things, meant that there were still many hurdles.

Warren says his next step was to collect information regarding the position of each member of the legislature who would be voting on the bill. Once he started getting the information, he also collected legislators' phone and fax numbers and put his plan in motion. He started by preparing a mass electronic mailing but took things slowly at first. "Because of the process, I didn't want to advocate hitting these legislators, these committee members with advocacy for the bill too early. So, I just queued up the message and started characterizing where each of the committee members stood," Warren explained. He made suggestions about how each legislator should be handled, how interested they were, and whom to pat on the back.

Then Warren added another touch. "I'd also include the zip code ranges for their districts so that anybody could ascertain who was in which zip code." Warren encouraged people to send copies of his e-mail to people they knew in zip codes where the legislators needed encouragement. The result was an outpouring of support, especially for a bill that many legislators had hoped would die quietly.

"Turns out that a very few people can have a lot of clout in a legislature," Warren observes. "I've been told that depending on the issue, it is not at all atypical for a member of the legislature to translate one letter into representing the view for anywhere from five to twenty-five thousand people."

Warren thinks that there are a number of reasons why the type of advocacy he used on the Internet works so well there. One of the reasons, the ability to be independent of time and place, has been mentioned before. Another important one is the fact that it is fast and easy to pass along communications, much more so than the traditional political tool, the telephone tree. "You don't have to worry about what the original message might be because it's come down through five levels of a phone tree," Warren notes, adding that when an e-mail message is forwarded, "you get the exact original communication. We have our own set of customs for adding our own annotations so that it is easy to track the process of a dialogue. It is a robust, established mechanism for the very fast, very cheap, exchange of information."

Warren notes that e-mail is particularly effective for volunteer and grass-roots organizations, both because of its cost and its flexibility. He adds that he thinks these capabilities will bring about more of what he calls "one shot activism," in which people will band together to back specific initiatives or issues.

One issue that Warren has been involved with more recently is the fight by many users of the Internet to overturn the Communications Decency Act, which was incorporated into the Telecommunications Act passed in early 1996. Warren used his mailing lists to follow the legislation step by step, and once it passed, to follow the subsequent court battles. Much of the protest to the legislation was generated by Warren's mailing lists.

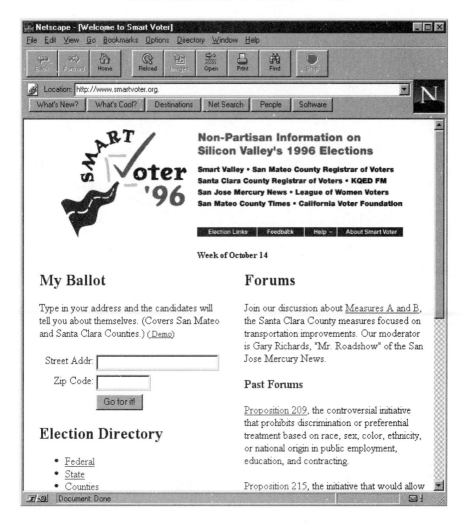

> Political activity on the nets during 1996 took a variety of forms. Some organizations, as shown here, used the Internet as a medium for providing information on the candidates running in local elections.

In his activities with the California legislature and later with the federal government, Warren took a fundamentally different approach than Pournelle in affecting legislation, but he was also effective. In Warren's case, he used his Internet capability as an enhancement to more traditional politics. In other words, he got the word out through e-mail, but once the word was passed, the response was handled through paper mail and faxes. There was no long-term organizational effort on line. In effect, Warren's "one shot activism" becomes an informal pressure group. In one sense, it is not unlike the ad hoc groups that form around a single issue, but these informal groups may not last any longer than required to register their feelings about the issue at hand and start changes moving.

In Warren's style of activism, the process works because the nets facilitate the formation of such short-term groups. In addition, Warren was careful not to use the capabilities of the nets for anything beyond what he knew would work. Again, the answer was not sophisticated technology and impressive graphics, but rather a dependable system that worked when it was needed. Here is what Warren found to work:

- **Communications immediacy.** Warren depended on his e-mail system to distribute alerts and information regarding the issue at hand. The e-mail contained enough information to allow interested members of Warren's list to take whatever action they desired, such as mailing a letter or sending a fax.

- **Communications accuracy.** By using e-mail, Warren was able to remain confident that the messages he sent out urging action were arriving intact. While some would have added comments by the users who had forwarded Warren's messages to their ultimate recipient, the original message would remain clear.

- **Political training.** Warren found that he was able to describe the actions he wanted his recipients to take, including providing addresses and fax numbers and suggestions for individually worded letters, which work better than form letters or postcards.

- **Limited objectives.** Warren asked his contacts to take a single action in support of a single issue. For this reason, when the people on his mailing list received his e-mail, all they were being asked to do was write and mail (or fax) a letter. Since the recipients were already sympathetic to the issue, his chances of success were good, and as a result his e-mail requests generated a relatively large number of letters. Because the legislators had not encountered this type of campaign before, they thought the numbers in support of Bowen's measure were quite high, and this helped ensure the bill's passage.

For Warren's campaign, e-mail became what the military refers to as a force multiplier. In other words, it makes your resources seem larger and more effective than they really are and in the process may give you greater capabilities. In this case, Warren's e-mail generated hundreds of letters, mainly from friends and contacts known to be inclined to support a cause in support of opening up the legislature. Since the legislature was inclined to think that letters were spontaneously generated, they operated under the assumption that each letter represented perhaps tens of thousands of voters. In such a way, a few hundred letters could translate into hundreds of thousands of potential votes. No legislature is likely to ignore such numbers.

Obviously, the U.S. Congress is not likely to ignore such numbers either, but in the case of the Congress, it takes larger numbers. According to Tanya Metaksa, director of the National Rifle Association's lobbying arm, the NRA routinely sends out alerts to members requesting letters to be written in support of the NRA's position on a particular issue. Like Warren, the NRA enjoys considerable success, because Congress also tends to translate letters into votes.

One significant feature about the e-mail messages sent out by Warren and by the NRA is that neither contains a suggested text for the letter they are asking people to write. Instead, the e-mail messages contain a point paper, a set of suggested positions, and a list of who should get the letters. The details are left up to the person receiving the e-mail. While not having a prepared text probably reduces the number of people who will send out letters, the fact that the letters received about a topic are obviously not form letters carries great weight. In a sense, these organizations trade a few points in numbers for significantly improved credibility.

In his research about political uses of the Internet, Mark Bonchek also noticed how the Internet is being used to enhance such organizational activities. He notes, for example, that many organizations use techniques similar to Warren's, although perhaps in a more institutionalized manner. "Amnesty International sends out electronic mail urging Action Alerts to notify members about political prisoners that have just been taken captive," Bonchek says, adding that such bulletins tell members to phone, fax, write, or to do something right away.

"That's a great use of the medium, nothing fancy, but it takes advantage of the fact that you can get rid of these space and time barriers and get a message out very quickly," Bonchek explains. "They take advantage of what I call the two-step flow, which is the use of the Internet to organize people who are politically active and on the net already into mobilizing and influencing Congress, government, whatever the target is, because then you get out of the limitations that those who are on the net are still only about 10 percent of the population."

The key to successful use of the Internet and on-line services is to take advantage of the medium's strengths, of course, but also to take advantage of its demographics. Because studies, including those of Bonchek, have shown that users of the nets tend to be more affluent, better educated, and more politically active than the population at large, the users are, as a group, likely to be interested in political events. Getting a response to a political need requires mostly that the proper group of users of the nets be targeted appropriately and asked to take a single action, such as writing a letter, that they would be inclined to take anyway. Nontraditional political groups, such as those with single-cause limited objective goals, are in a position to dramatically multiply their apparent forces by using the nets and a carefully targeted selection of recipients.

▶ Spontaneous Political Actions

During 1995 a number of congressional offices faced a perplexing new protest. Their fax machines were churning out paper, their e-mail boxes were being filled (for those few who had e-mail), and the phones were ringing constantly. This is not an unusual event when Congress is considering a controversial bill. In this case, however, the confusion mounted. The problem was that the letters, faxes, and phone calls were strongly protesting what the writers alleged was planned legislation that would make it a federal offense to drink while driving on the information superhighway. Thousands of users, many of whom apparently would open a brew while they surfed the Net, were outraged. After all, what business was it of the government if they wanted a tall cool one while they looked for cool new Web sites?

The answer, of course, is that it was not the government's business at all. In fact, there was no such legislation planned at all. The belief that there might be was the result of a phony, but authentic looking, news story that was posted to an Internet newsgroup. Even though it was revealed as a hoax almost immediately, letters and calls arrived for days. The result was an annoyed set of staffers bemused by the protest and a somewhat lower opinion of Internet users. While the events that led to the protest about drinking on the information superhighway were false, the results are important, because they demonstrate that Internet users are willing and able to form spontaneous groups almost immediately to counter a threat, real or imagined.

Just such a threat appeared in January 1996, when Congress passed the Telecommunications Act of 1996, into which was incorporated the provisions of an earlier bill, the Communications Decency Act, which had been defeated by Congress when it was presented on its own. Internet users were especially outraged, and they vented their anger by flooding Congress with letters, faxes, and phone calls. Unfortunately, because the provisions of the Decency Act were inserted into the telecommunications bill as an amendment and the bill was quickly passed, the protest took place too late for it to do any good.

Part of the protest effort, however, resulted in a number of organizations and individuals agreeing to fight the act in court together. Shortly after the January signing of the act, the government was enjoined from enforcing it because of the legal action brought by the group that formed spontaneously to fight it. While much of the impetus to objections to this bill came from messages generated by Jim Warren, the group was already well on its way to coalescing by the time Warren's Government Access mailing list started pushing it in earnest.

When the challenges to the Communications Decency Act were heard in federal court during the summer of 1996, the groups fighting it were successful, at least initially. The special three-judge panel, meeting in Philadelphia, upheld their challenge. In addition, the court blocked enforcement of the act by the Department of Justice and granted First Amendment protection to the Internet and private on-line services. In the fall of 1996, however, the Department of Justice announced that it would appeal the finding to the U.S. Supreme Court, which plans to hear the case in 1997.

▶ On the Political Fringe

For some groups, pressuring Congress through fax and e-mailings is far too mainstream. There are groups that either do not believe in the legitimacy of the legislature or who believe that as people they are so corrupt that appeals to reason will not work. For some such groups, the preferred method to explain their position is through organized protests.

The problem with such an approach is that except in towns with large student populations, it is sometimes difficult to find enough people interested in protest as a way to influence government. Worse, even when such people can be found, it is hard to plan and execute something as logistically complex as a major protest. Even small protest demonstrations require the involvement of people and, ultimately, communications between people. It is in planning and communicating the details that alternative groups join the mainstream in using the nets as efficient means of getting the word out to their members and sympathizers and to like-minded groups that may want to get involved.

One such effort, for example, is run by Jennifer Angel (a pseudonym; her real last name is Engle, and you'll learn more about her in Chapter 5), an activist and publisher of Internet mailing lists aimed at anarchists and people with related interest who runs a sort of clearinghouse and Internet mailing list containing a regularly updated list of planned protests and music festivals for people involved in alternative politics. Her e-mail list, which is handled much as a newsletter would be in a print environment, is really a collection of announcements from other interested groups announcing their activities, looking for participants for protest demonstrations, or passing on information to others who may be compiling such information.

Unlike many such lists, Angel's is highly interactive. She actively requests reader input and publishes requests for contributions from other groups. While the list is also available on the Web, it is through the use of the mailing list features of the Internet e-mail system that she makes her greatest impact, in large part by her involvement with user participation. For example, her e-mail announced protests at the Republican National Convention in San Diego while asking for more details on the convention and on planned protests.

Where the groups in Angel's mailing list also share similarity with the other, more mainstream groups is that they have no sure way of knowing the impact of their e-mailed requests. They are, in effect, depending on careful targeting and on the fact that recipients will forward her messages to others they know with similar interests. In one sense, it is here that another characteristic of the nets rises to importance. Participants tend to ask for information that they are interested in receiving. Thus, requested mailing lists are much like controlled circulation publications, which means that the recipients are more highly qualified as readers than the general public.

The presence of highly qualified readers, whether for planning protests or selling magazine advertising, is a substantial asset. Because the interests of the readers can be gauged by their requests for material, so can their motivation to act on the material once it is received. While not everyone will act on every message, a higher percentage than the normal population of net users will, and that justifies the effort to maintain a political mailing list.

The tendency to attract qualified readers is especially useful for informal, ad hoc, and alternative political groups, because these groups are frequently not part of the normal coverage picture for traditional media. The lack of coverage may be due to several factors, including low numbers or nontraditional doctrine (meaning the media does not understand them), or they may remain out of the traditional media by choice. In many cases, these groups believe—often with some justification—that their opponents base their view of the world strictly on traditional media, and, as a result, by staying away, they effectively remain invisible.

Normally, one associates visibility as a desirable feature in politics but that depends on the organization. In situations where a group is trying to leverage its technical knowledge into a force multiplier, it is best to stay out of the glare of publicity and let the results of their efforts speak for themselves. As long as the results are all that appears, the target of those efforts will continue to believe that the groups are larger, more active, or better funded than they really are. As long as they believe that, the goals of the organizations using the nets as a force multiplier are met. It is only when the target finds out the true nature of the organization that the goals are at risk, not necessarily because the group or their goals are at odds with legislative desires, but rather because it then becomes obvious that there is less there than meets the eye.

In a sense, these informal groups can use the nets and their base of electronic communications as a sort of guerrilla warfare, in the sense that politics and the use of information forms a type of verbal and procedural warfare. Many of the same techniques are used, including misdirection, concealment, and informal operations. Here, of course, they involve political rather than military operations, but ultimately the goals are the same—a change in the way government works. In this type of political operation, however, the organizations are temporary or unofficial, but results can be significant.

cape

lt View Go Bookmarks Options Directory Window Help

Home   Reload   Open   Print   Find   Stop

letsite: http://www.democrats.org/

t's New?   What's Cool?   Destinations   Net Search   People   Software

5

N

Radical and Fringe
Politics on the Nets

"The major thing that I notice, because it makes transaction costs so cheap, is that it opens up the possibility of organizing in ways that haven't been opened before," explains the Democratic National Committee's Dick Bell. "It makes it a lot easier for insurgent forces of whatever sort to organize than ever before." Bell is not the only political operative on the Internet who has noticed that the cost and difficulty of entry is easily overcome. In fact, if any force in American politics has leveled the playing field for the traditional major political parties and groups with views somewhat outside the mainstream, it is the presence of the nets.

"This is a way that everyone can get their voice out there," explains Jennifer Engle, a student at Ohio State University and distributor (under the name Jen Angel) of a number of politically oriented mailing lists. Engle, who considers herself aligned with groups in the midwestern United States that are proponents of anarchism and collectivism, says that her activities would be very difficult to carry out without access to the nets. More important, however, she thinks the existence of the nets is critical for a true marketplace of ideas. "It means that the smallest person, the smallest Web page, can get publicity, can get heard, which I think is excellent," Engle notes.

Her most widely distributed mailing list is her conferences list, a periodic list of the meetings of people and groups who are involved in what they term "progressive politics."

These groups, or collectives, also frequently hold meetings in conjunction with major political events. In August 1996, for example, Engle was involved with organizing a conference of political activists during the Democratic National Convention in Chicago. "More specifically, a conference in August in Chicago called Active Resistance, which surrounded the Democratic National Convention."

"All the collectives try to make it easier to communicate with each other and to give each other mutual aid." Engle continues, describing how she and others use the nets for their planning and communications and "getting that out to the other collectives." Such organizing activities are critical for the groups Engle writes for and to which she distributes her lists. Because the numbers involved are fairly small and the individuals who work with them are so spread out, communications can be a real problem.

The Internet provides the means for Engle to collect the details of the conferences she covers in her mailing list. "I use it in a lot of different ways," Engle says. "I use it to stay aware of things that are going on, because it is really up to date, like to the minute, as opposed to waiting for newsletters to come out. A lot of the mailing lists that I'm on post news-oriented articles. I also use it to stay in contact with people, especially because it saves making long distance phone calls, and with the Network Anarchist Collectives, it's a really good tool to keep in touch, . . . [and] to supplement what we do outside, because we know that not everybody has e-mail access even though we want them to. . . . We're using e-mail and the Net in a couple of different ways," Engle explains. "We're using that because the Network [Anarchist Collectives] is so spread out. We're using the net to keep in touch with each other about what's going on so in that way we are coordinating with other organizers and we're also doing outreach."

Engle notes, for example, that her mailing lists and the lists of others frequently overlap, so that everyone gets all of the information they need. "Because I'm personally involved with the Chicago Conference, I'll put announcements for it on my other list. And there's announcements for Chicago because it's something I'm personally involved with, and I'll also talk it up when I'm in newsgroups or to other people I know on e-mail. So I use it both for organizing and coordination with other people and for outreach."

Adding to the complexity of organizing the activities of the groups Engle is involved with is that many of them operate internationally. For groups that cannot afford long distance phone calls, conducting overseas activities might otherwise be impossible without the nets. Add that to the number of people involved with these groups, and the nature of their problem becomes obvious. If they are to exist, they must use the nets. As Engle explains, "I use [the Internet] because it is an inexpensive way to get out a lot of information to a lot of people at once."

Engle's activities are typical of smaller, less traditional groups that do not have the membership numbers to get noticed. Instead, they must be able to communicate efficiently, act quickly, and use technology to substitute for people and money. In some areas, the results have been significant. One good example is the Piedmont Environmental Council, an environmentalist and antidevelopment group that was responsible for organizing resistance to a proposed Disney theme park in Prince William County in northern Virginia. Government officials knew that there were few opponents to the "Disney's America," scheduled to open in the late 1990s. What those officials did not know was that environmentalists, along with sympathetic preservationists, were ready to act. *Washington Post* staff writers Stephen C. Fehr and Eric Lipton described (May 27, 1996) the problem facing the Prince William County government as "the sophistication of the residents battling development who now organize and communicate with decision-makers through e-mail, fax and voice mail. The growth of homeowners associations has added a new force. 'Now you can create the impression of a huge movement through the use of information technology,' said Prince William County Executive James H. Mullen."

Chris Miller, head of the Piedmont Environmental Council, a land-use group, recalled a recent meeting of Prince William and Fauquier county residents battling plans for highway and rail projects: "Someone asked who can do a computer database with names and addresses, and five hands went up. Then it was, who can put together a Web site? Two hands went up. Who has experience with environmental impact statements?" Three environmental engineers raised their hands.

While some might question calling such groups as the Piedmont Environmental Council radical, there is little question that they were so considered by the Disney executives and county officials who tried to fight them. Regardless, they use the same techniques as and display the same level of sophistication of many small, politically active groups, and they had a direct effect on (or were at least the catalyst for) the cancellation of the park.

▶ Hate on the Net

A number of activist groups have noticed that in addition to like-minded groups getting on line, so are their opponents. The range of groups matches that of the full political spectrum, from the far right to the far left, all using many of the same techniques and sometimes saying much the same things.

Internet activist Jim Warren, publisher of the Internet-based newsletter GovAccess, which addresses such items as access to government records and information and the access by the government to private records and private on-line communications, says: "One of the things that we're finding that is happening more and more, to the great distress of established authorities and established power bases, is that all of these weird little eccentric groups are gaining the ability to organize. Why? Because they can identify themselves. It doesn't make any difference if they are scattered all over the nation. You know, whether it's the white supremacists or the flat earthers or the radical environmentalists, all these little constituencies that never could organize themselves before because they simply couldn't identify themselves have now been able to start finding each other."

Warren, who has been politically active on the Internet for years and is the founder of the West Coast Computer Faire, says that the Internet is a natural home for many groups that operate outside the mainstream. The reason, of course, is that the powerful indexing and search capabilities of the commercial search engines, such as Yahoo and AltaVista, make finding nearly anything easy.

"Just go into Yahoo and ask," Warren says, suggesting that it is possible to find discussions and Web sites for any topic you like, even if the only information is a discussion in the Internet newsgroups. "There is going to be a discussion of it, and you are able to establish linkups and start to build a constituency that was never possible before, and they are able to continue communications, which was never economically possible before because it cost too much to publish a magazine for only five hundred people. So, in a since, I think that will further contribute to the fragmentation of traditional politics. But it also will contribute to, for better or for worse, honest democratization."

At this point, Warren's thoughts about fragmentation seem to play a greater role than democratization. One reason is that many groups that operate on the political fringes are not necessarily all that interested in sharing their beliefs with the uninitiated. For them, such things as Web sites and public discussions smack of inadequate security. Interestingly, it is the lack of security that has kept some organizations off the public networks entirely. The really militant groups, the militias and the like, appear to restrict their communications to bulletin board services where access can be carefully controlled. On the other hand, many groups that used to be fairly secretive, including white supremacists, communists, and anti-Semitic groups, are now well represented on the World Wide Web.

The result of easy and inexpensive access is that nearly any group can have a worldwide communications medium at their fingertips. This easy access means that groups such as Engle's can stay on line, even if it is only by using electronic mail to their university accounts. It also means that the level and nature of political activity can be very broad. For example, in the fall of 1996, CIA Director John Deutch revealed in a Washington news conference that his agency was watching the activities of terrorists from the Middle East, who once had used phones and were now using the Internet to plan their activities.

Meanwhile, many groups that might once have been shrouded in mystery now are quite open about their activities. Not only are the conferences and collectives that Engle works with becoming more active through their mailing lists, many such groups are publicly presenting their views on their Web sites. This turn of events is having unexpected effects. For example, the Anti-Defamation League is now spending much more money and time on producing content for Web sites that affirm the reality of the Holocaust, if only to combat the dozens of sites of groups that maintain it never happened.

▶ Using the Nets for Action

Groups that are politically out of the mainstream follow much the same pattern as traditional political groups when it comes to their Internet activities. Of course, there are differences. An examination of their mailing list content material shows that these groups rely much more heavily on the nets for organizational activities, mainly because of physical requirements.

After all, the reason these groups are not part of the mainstream is because there are relatively few members who ascribe to their political positions. As Jim Warren explains, they need the Internet or a commercial on-line service as a way to find each other and as a way to make plans, handle logistics, and recruit new members. Whereas a larger group might hold a meeting, many of these groups can never meet with any regularity because of both distance and financial constraints. As a result, much of the information that moves between members of the group is organizational in nature, including such material as planned gatherings, meetings, or events in conjunction with other events, or the preparation of materials or Internet postings.

Another large component of the material that passes between members as part of their mailing lists is political discussion. Most of these smaller groups are acutely aware of their size compared to larger established organizations. One means they have of continuing to build community spirit as well as attract new members is to discuss their political views with likely members.

Education and outreach is also an important component of the activities of politically active groups. For example, most of the conferences that Engle mentions are educational efforts in which members of like-minded organizations are taught the basics of one form or another of their particular brand of activism. In Engle's case, it is anarchism and collectivism, but it could be anything, depending on the group.

Examples of such education and outreach cover the spectrum of activities that smaller groups are likely to need as a way to tell their story. During the research for this book we found mailing-list references for training sessions on Internet Activism, distribution of radical graphics and art, congressional lobbying, and media relations. Other topics uncovered on newsgroups and Web sites range from food distribution to how to get literature printed cheaply (find a Xerox Corporation repair person and get that person to join the group to print radical posters as test pages).

One interesting aspect of education and outreach is that it seems more prevalent in groups that classify themselves as being on the left politically. We found, for example, that some Web sites, notably the Institute for Global Communications (http://www.igc.org) in

Palo Alto, California, provide links to dozens of organizations involved in issues from antinuclear protests to labor and women's issues. The list runs from Amnesty International to Zero Population Growth. We did not find a similar site that identifies itself as part of the far right.

▶ News and Politics

One area that seems to be part of all Internet activity conducted by radical and fringe groups is the provision of a source of news specific to the interests of the group. To some extent this is because the news carried on their mailing lists is primarily related to their organization. In addition, however, many of these groups do not appear to believe that the traditional news media will accurately reflect their views. They have what amounts to their own news wire services, because they do not believe they will hear about events important to them any other way.

Depending on the group, these news items range from reports on congressional hearings on such subjects as privacy issues, priests jailed for protesting on U.S. Army bases, and the arrest of protesters at the Democratic National Convention. That last item is typical of many of the urgent messages that flow through the e-mail networks operated by many such groups. Messages about arrests at the 1996 convention usually began, "URGENT ALERT!! Spread Widely and Quickly." Through these messages the word continued to spread about the arrest of a news crew from CounterMedia, a collective of media activists. The group was associated with Active Resistance, which was organizing some of the protests during the Democratic convention in Chicago. Similar messages during the convention on other mailing lists included the arrests of activists, alleged terrorists, journalists, and politicians. There were also news articles on environmental issues, animal rights and health issues. The alerts and urgent news covered the spectrum of issues from all sides.

▶ Fund-raising

Like their larger cousins—the major political parties—the less mainstream organizations need funding, and they frequently use their best communications facility—the nets—as a way to get it. Jennifer

Engle reports that her mailing list is frequently used for fund-raising for the groups she supports, as well as a way to help pay for the costs of supporting her mailing list.

"If you look at just the contributions I get," Engle says, explaining how one of her mailing lists raises funds successfully, "the conference list is international, and I've got contributions from England and Scotland and Germany, all over Europe, in South America, in the Caribbean, as well as, of course, America and Canada." Engle says that the contributions demonstrate the international reach of her mailing list, where the messages are frequently forwarded from one user to another, far beyond the original list of addressees. "That shows me that a lot of people are reading it from those areas," Engle explains, "and also, because a lot of the lists, like the Anarchist List, tend to not be American, centered on America."

Engle's global fund-raising reach helps support more than just the mailing list she works with and more than just the organizations she supports. Because her list is often incorporated into other mailing lists, her material also supports other efforts, which also gather funds to support their own activities.

▶ Supporting the Citizen Activist

While members of groups on the political fringes may make good use of the nets as a way to organize protests, and as a way to meet others of like minds, can it lead anywhere? In fact, it can. As was the case with the Piedmont Environmental Council, citizens with a strong belief in an issue can use the nets to make their presence felt, even if the issue is not particularly popular or widely shared.

As Jim Warren points out, the nets are particularly well-suited for helping people who normally would not be able to participate in such political activities find a home and take part in the debate, even if they cannot do so personally. In addition, the organizational possibilities extend beyond just getting people to vote or attend rallies.

"It has a robust established mechanism for very cheap, very fast exchange of information, broadcast of information, and facilitation of organization," Warren points out, "yet it facilitates fast response teams. It is particularly useful for volunteer groups. That is for-real honest grass-roots activism. Initially because of its cost, but notably because of its 'different time, different place' capabilities." Warren says that because of the time-shifting ability of the nets that allows people to carry on conversations in something other than real time, the nets avoid shutting people out who work odd shifts or spend long hours commuting. "I'm traveling all over the state," Warren says as an example. "How can anybody keep track of me or get in touch with me? Easy. Send the stuff to my e-mail box. So, honest grass-roots activism is empowered in ways that have never before been possible."

So what do groups with less traditional political views do on the nets? Pretty much the same things everyone else does, but the mix is different. For these groups, cost and simplicity are critical issues, because their members are often operating out of accounts provided through universities or free networks, where facilities often are not up to the levels of commercial Internet service providers. As a result, there are relatively fewer elaborate Web sites and more use of e-mail and mailing lists and more discussion on Internet newsgroups.

On the other hand, the charges by many on the left that the right-wing groups have the best Web sites is belied by experience. While there are many groups on the left who cannot afford anything elaborate (and for whom elaborate sites are counter to their philosophy), there are many more, including the Institute for Global Communications or the International Workers of the World (http://www.iww.org), that are as elaborate and well-designed as any other political site. Still, the view persists. "From what I know, the far right has had better-looking Web sites up faster than the folks at our end of the scale," Karen Wickre complained to the *San Francisco Examiner* in June 1996. Wickre, founder of Digital Queers, helps gay and lesbian groups get on line as a way to get their message out.

Perhaps because of the efforts of Wickre and others, as well as the dramatic growth of political activity on the nets in general, both ends of the political spectrum appear to be reaching parity in the battle of the Web pages. In any case, the differences in how these groups use the nets appears to be more related to a group's philosophy about how resources should be expended and how much budget is available than to basic knowledge or creativity.

▶ The Net and Radical Politics

A list of uses for the nets in radical and fringe politics looks a lot like a list for any other type of political use. What is more important is the emphasis, whether it is for public relations, recruitment, member communications, or fund-raising. Here's a look at the differences:

- **Public relations.** Virtually every political group on the nets recognizes the public relations aspect of being able to tell their story. This is why groups such as the Aryan Nations (http://stormfront.wat.com/stormfront/an.htm) and Digital Queers (http://www.dq.org) have home pages on the Internet that provide basic organizational information, statements of their purpose, and contact information. This is, of course, also a way to avoid filtering by the media, a theme that seems to persist throughout radical and fringe political organizations that use the nets.

- **Recruitment.** One of the most significant aspects of the nets for smaller political organizations is the ability of people of like minds to find each other. By having some sort of activity on the nets, especially a home page on the Web, such groups can be located and contacted by potential members.

- **Member communications.** Most of the nationwide and international groups involved with radical and fringe politics would not be able to exist in their current form without the nets. The availability of cheap, fast, and effective communications with their membership allows them to exist when they would otherwise be too thinly spread to exist. In addition, as a number of government officials and advocates have noted, the ability to communicate quickly allows a group to appear large, well-funded, and well-organized, regardless of whether that is actually the case.

- **Media relations.** One of the attractions of the nets is that it provides a pathway to the mass media for organizations that need one. While not all fringe or radical organizations want media attention (believing that the media is part of the establishment), many do, at least as a way to report on abuses of their rights.

- **Fund-raising.** Most radical organizations share two characteristics: they are chronically short of money, and they are not required to report to the Federal Election Commission. This means that fund-raising can be an informal activity, well-suited to the nets. In fact, getting funds for operation of her mailing lists and the organizations she supports is a major activity of Jennifer Engle and others with similar purposes.

- **Group communications.** While groups on the political left appear to do more group-to-group communicating than those on the right, communications among groups with compatible goals is an important use of the nets and one that appears to be increasing as groups learn that by working together, they can create the appearance of being larger than they are.
- **Political discussions.** Until recently, the practice of carrying on wide-ranging political discussions was largely the province of the fringe and radical groups. In 1996, however, the Republicans adopted this practice very successfully with the forms that the GOP linked to its Web page. For fringe and radical groups, such discussions are an important part of self-identification and a way to recruit potential members. In addition, they also serve to shore up morale by helping members of these thinly scattered organizations realize that they are not fighting their battles alone.

One effect of this access to the new media is that many smaller, more radical groups are becoming more like their mainstream cousins, at least in public. In fact, it may be that one of the great leveling effects of the nets is the need to appear generally acceptable as a way to get the public to read an organization's Web site. While this level of public relations sophistication worries some—usually the left worries that the groups on the right are getting too good at their Web pages, while groups on the right worry about the left and their Web pages—less impassioned observers appear to feel that access to the nets is actually encouraging democracy.

Jim Warren is one of those, and he has been involved with activism on the net for years. Many of his activities are completely mainstream, while others move more to the fringes of the political spectrum. Warren's involvement in the fight on the Internet against the Communications Decency Act of 1996 was one of the events that brought him into the public spotlight. Warren, however, has been a prime force in the efforts to use the nets as a political medium, because he says he feels that it helps bring government into the hands of more people, if only because it is easier that way.

"It is very difficult to maintain a constituency over time that has very much power," Warren notes, explaining why creating pressure groups and political parties has always been difficult. "The party structure and the old party boss structure in local politics—ward politics—used to work because there was a payback. You do this for us and we'll pay you back. We'll pay you for your votes at election time. And for your get-out-the-vote effort. But that's pretty much fallen by the wayside in most jurisdictions, most districts.

"Now along comes the net and it turns out that it is very easy to build a constituency for a given topic. Suddenly, I don't have to invest a huge amount of time, effort, and resources into creating a constituency. I can create it fast, I can create it widespread, and I can create it very inexpensively for a given topic. There is no infrastructure charge and there is very little delay. That means that you can build a constituency very fast and very viably for a given topic, which means that you don't have to maintain a permanent constituency."

"This empowers grass-roots activism, as opposed to the necessity in the older days, the pre-networking days, of having ward politics and having party politics and having established parties focused on a whole array of issues because that was the only way that you could build a constituency in the first place," Warren notes, suggesting that over the long run the political landscape could change and in the process open up the debate to more views and more organizations. "And I think that over time we are going to see this have a substantial impact on the way politics operates in every first-world nation that allows free, unfettered communications."

Jennifer Engle agrees with Warren and puts a very Jeffersonian twist to it. The nets, she believes, form the new home for the marketplace of ideas Jefferson treasured, where all views can be heard and minds made up. "A lot of people talk about the marketplace of ideas and how that designates us from the U.S. [establishment], because there is no access to the media and the media is only accessible to a certain number of groups," Engle explains, pointing out the disenfranchisement felt by many members of radical and fringe political groups. "If a lot of people have access to the Internet and to the Web, that's kind of training that marketplace. So, I'd like to see people take advantage of that and use it for discussion and not spouting off about what [their] ideas are. I'd like to see real discussion of things, and I'd also like it to be more information-oriented. So even though I like the discussion, I would like to see more information.

"I'm all in favor of anyone putting their ideas out there whether I disagree with them or not, because the more ideas out there, the more people can judge for themselves, especially if everything is out there and you can counter things and if there is discussion that goes along with it." Engle explains that for her and members of the groups she works with, it is the access to information and opinions, regardless of their slant, that matters. "I think it's all fine," she says.

The reality of the nets seems to be that as groups that once seemed to be completely beyond normal politics come into closer contact with the mainstream, they also change to more closely reflect the mainstream. In the meantime, the opposite also appears to be taking place, that as the mainstream learns more about some of the views of the fringe and radical political groups, the more it embraces some of their ideas, if not all of their practices.

A number of observers have suggested that the nets are playing a key role in opening democracy up to a much wider range of people. It would also seem that the nets are playing an equally important role in bringing groups that once were beyond the edge of democracy into the larger community. Whether this spreading of the mainstream is good or not depends on one's beliefs. On one hand, there are many who belong to the fringe specifically because they wish to reject the mainstream, and for them such a trend only means that their options are growing fewer. On the other hand, for groups that have a specific agenda or that have goals they want to see adopted, this broader access can bring only good, because their ideas will take their place in the broader marketplace and will stand or fall on their own accord.

Ultimately, both Engle and Warren are right in their belief that greater access will ultimately be positive for the goals of their groups, whether it is for civil liberties or collectivism. Their views will be available so that they can be fully understood and appreciated by anyone who is interested. Whether the mainstream agrees or not is then up to the reader. The groups, at least, will have had their say in the arena of public opinion.

It is, in fact, the attraction to what is essentially a free marketplace of ideas that makes the nets so interesting to the politically active. In effect, anyone anywhere can hold any view they wish and publish it. As is the case in any other forum, there is no guarantee that anyone will agree with those ideas, or even listen to them, but the fact that any idea can be published is inescapable.

What is potentially more important is that the views of individuals and small groups are given much more weight than they would have in any other medium. While the major political parties and larger organizations may have a more elaborate presence on the Internet, the fact is that nearly anyone can put up a site on the Web and maintain it. This means that people searching for viewpoints on a topic of their choice will have the opportunity to see every group's position on that topic, not just the views of the major groups. In effect, the nets have become a sort of virtual village green, on which any idea can be discussed and addressed on its merits. It has become, in effect, the embodiment of the ideal of the marketplace of ideas.

Group-to-Group Communications and the International Connection

"The net is a marvelous organizing vehicle," Professor David Farber says, explaining how groups can use the easy and inexpensive communications of the nets as a way to work together. Farber notes that the Internet is especially fertile ground for groups, from radical activists and splinter groups to more traditional members of the political process, to learn about each other and, in some cases, work together. "You can actually make things work now with very small groups of people communicating with each other over the net in very tactical ways," Farber says. He thinks that the ability of groups to work together cooperatively without the constraints of either time or location could change the political process in a number of important ways. Of course, to do that the groups have to find each other and learn to work together. "Domestically and internationally, a lot of that goes on now—it makes sense," Farber says.

Professor Farber, who holds an endowed chair in telecommunications at the University of Pennsylvania, thinks that the nets are a perfect place for the formation of politically active groups, whether they work in a specific country or function internationally. He says that the speed, moderate expense, and flexibility of the nets all stand to make group interaction a sure thing, and, to some extent, a thing that is already there.

Farber, among others, also says that the role of international communications among groups is sure to grow. This is because there are no effective borders for the messages that flow across the nets, and, as a result, there is no reason why political activities need to be restricted to a specific state or nation. This means that on the nets at least, politics is on its way to becoming international in scope, instead of local, as traditional political activity has always been.

As Jennifer Engle found out when she started getting donations and help from Internet users outside the United States, political activity in the United States is a subject of intense interest around the world. Engle, in her efforts to spread information about anarchist and collective group activities using her mailing lists, attracted the attention of other groups with similar interests in other countries. Of course, Engle is by no means alone in discovering this. Internet supervisors from every party and pressure group find many reasons to have regular contact with individuals and groups overseas, and the overseas users actively contact them.

Part of the reason, of course, is that there is frequently a great commonality of interest among political groups worldwide. On a more practical basis, the election cycle is different in the United States than it is in Europe or Asia, and political activists there can watch what works in the United States and plan their activities accordingly. Likewise, U.S. political managers keep a keen eye on overseas activities as elections develop there.

"We do have visits and for a long time have had visits from domains in other countries," says Jim Manown, a communications specialist and spokesperson for the National Rifle Association (NRA) Institute for Legislative Action (ILA). Manown is in charge of the NRA's extensive Web site on the Internet, keeps track of where visitors are from, and passes requests for information to others at that organization. He says the people and organizations that come by include visits from Europe, Eastern Europe, Russia, Asia, South and Central America, and Australia.

Manown works for NRA-ILA Executive Director Tanya Metaksa, who says that a number of firearms groups in other countries look to the NRA for leadership. Of course, the major political parties also get a great deal of interest from outside the United States. "Obviously the vast majority of hits on the [Republican National Committee] site come from the United States," says Jonathan Knisley, who runs the Republican Web site, "but we have had membership requests from Bosnia. We've gotten them from Australia, Canada, you know, sort of everywhere. Because of FEC [Federal Election Committee] rules, we can't take contributions from foreign nationals so that doesn't do us a whole lot of good, but it's somewhat interesting that those people are interested in joining the Republican Party and are obviously visiting our site. You know, we have had hits from Estonia, Czechoslovakia, just sort of all over the world. We've had a couple from South Africa. You know, it's intriguing that those different areas are interested in what we are doing."

The interest from overseas extends to the manner in which politically active groups make use of the nets. In the United Kingdom, for example, activity by the major political parties parallels that of party activity in the United States. In Great Britain the apparent tendency for the more conservative political party to have a more comprehensive site on the World Wide Web appears to hold.

The Conservative Party Web site (http://www.conservative-party. org.uk/), while not using the graphical motif of the Republicans in the United States, does make heavy use of animated graphics, video, and audio. There is a clear, very friendly area aimed at students, and there are links to other conservative organizations, as well as to regional offices of the Conservative Party.

The Labour Party (http://www.poptel.org.uk/labour-party/), by contrast, has only limited support for animation or multimedia, and its site is somewhat more limited. Perhaps more important, however, the Labour Party provides e-mail addresses to important areas within the party, which the Conservative Party does not. Here, the Labour Party clearly has gone to the trouble to set up electronic-mail accounts for various offices in the party and allows voters and the media to contact them directly.

The British government has also opened for business on the nets in the United Kingdom. As is the case with the site for the U.S. Congress, visitors to the U.K. site can get information on pending actions in Parliament, gain access to documents, and check into the activities of cabinet departments. While the information on the site (http://www.parliament.uk/) is fairly dry, it is comprehensive and more open than some observers expected it to be.

Perhaps the British government is following the lead of the European Commission, which has been on line for years and has been aggressive in making information on and access to the European Union's institutions a priority. The Web site of the European Commission (http://europa.eu.int/) has vast archives, as well as a wide collection of current information from sites around the world. For current users of the Internet and, to a lesser extent, the commercial on-line services, the activity on the European Commission's Web site, especially the site aimed at issues involving the Internet specifically—the Information Society Project Office (http://www.ispo.cec.be/)—can be very important. Much of the activity involving content and copyright issues that ultimately become part of treaty negotiations begins here. While the contents of the European Commission's site are quite dry, when compared to other sites, it is a good place to start looking for people involved with the political future of the nets, because it can eventually become the source for laws that attempt to control the political expression and content of net users everywhere.

▶ Group Connections

"Amnesty International sends out electronic mail urging Action Alerts to notify members about political prisoners that have just been taken captive, and they'll send out a bulletin that says phone, fax, write, do something right away," says MIT researcher Mark Bonchek in describing one politically active group that operates internationally. In fact, Amnesty International is part of a worldwide network of organizations that work together to support each others efforts. At the same time, Amnesty International works with groups in individual countries that are attempting to support its goal of eliminating human rights abuses.

"When you connect with someone's Web page now," explains Democratic Congresswoman Anna Eshoo, who represents the Fourteenth District in California, "there is almost an automatic trigger from the Republic National Committee to other like organizations or issues groups that come around with their issues." Eshoo is one of the most active members of Congress on the nets and is acutely aware of the role they play both in affecting elections and in legislation. The trend she sees in the United States is also reflected elsewhere, as groups try to band together to share like interests and find support around the world.

One of the reasons that the nets are so effective in helping build support for such group interaction is that the nets know no national borders, which means that the Labour Party in the United Kingdom and the Democratic Party in the United States can share ideas over the nets and elsewhere, learning from each other what works, and trade information on issues of mutual interest.

Of course, there are limits. In the United States and in many other countries, foreign nationals are not supposed to be involved in national elections or in the national political process, which means that groups that are officially sanctioned have to be careful who is playing an active role and who is contributing money. Thus, many groups in the United States concentrate their group-to-group activities on domestic organizations, rather than devoting resources on international contacts.

A number of linked sites on the Internet are combined to form a vast network of political activity on the nets. The core of one such site is the Institute for Global Communications (http://www.igc. org/), which provides links to dozens of progressive sites and other Internet resources usually (but not exclusively) of interest to people who support the political left. For example, one of the links in IGC's list will take a user to Amnesty International USA (http:// www.amnesty-usa.org/). Others, including Friends of the Earth (http://www.essential.org/FOE.html), provide their own pages of links to organizations they feel share a common interest. Therefore, it can take only two steps to go from IGC's massive list of organizations to the Piedmont Environmental Council (http://www.pec-va.org/), a local group in Prince William County, Virginia, near Washington, D.C., that formed to fight a proposed Disney theme park and continues to fight development in the area.

Many of the organizations featured in the IGC list operate internationally. Some, especially some of the organizations formed to protect fragile environmental areas, operate overseas but solicit support in the United States. On the other hand, some organizations are intended to operate globally. One such organization with an important presence on the Internet is the Industrial Workers of the World (who call themselves the "Wobblies"). The IWW (http:// www.iww.org/hall/) uses its Internet site to recruit members and to promote causes, but it also uses its presence to provide publicity and Internet links to what it calls Anarchist and Labor Resources on the World Wide Web. These resources include such groups as the Communist Party USA, the European Counter Network, Red and Anarchist SkinHeads, and the Socialist Party USA Cybercenter. Many of the sites and resources listed by the IWW have their own links, some leading back and others leading to yet more related organizations.

Perhaps the most ambitious of these sites is the National Political Index (http://www.politicalindex.com/), which, in an effort to reach political activists as well as journalists and people interested in politics, has links to more than 3,500 sites on the Internet. While there are political sites that are not available through the National Political Index, there are not many, and despite the large number of groups listed with the National Political Index, international activity and overseas listings appear to be only incidental.

Interestingly, conservative groups also seem to concentrate on U.S. domestic issues and groups and to ignore international connections. While groups identifying with the political right have an extensive network of mutual links throughout the Internet, connections to groups outside the United States are essentially nonexistent. What information does exist regarding overseas activities normally appears on the pages of links that include other groups, a few of which may have overseas connections.

▶ The Conservative Connection

Conservative groups in the United States are well-represented on the nets. Their Web sites on the Internet are slick, complete, and have many links to other sites of likely interest to people interested in conservative issues. For the most part, these groups are well-organized and tend to congregate around core Web sites from which links lead to nearly everywhere that appeals to conservative users. Two of those sites, The Conservative Link (http://www.powerpark.com/ bmdesign/TCL) and Town Hall (http://www.townhall. com/) illustrate how conservatives in the United States use the Internet.

What is interesting is that the avoidance of international connections appears to be intentional, as it is in the case of The Conservative Link, which is run as a hobby by Jeff Williams, a Web Page designer from Pullman, Washington. Williams reports that he

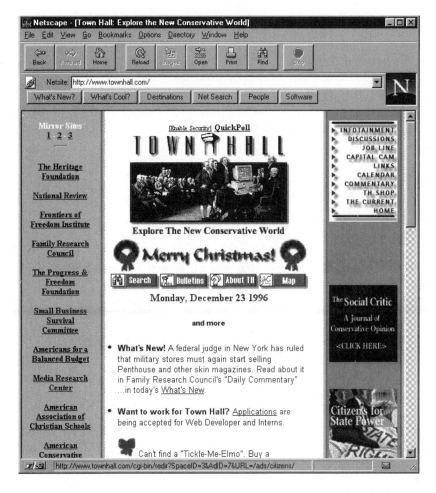

> Town Hall provides a broad selection of links to other conservative groups, as well as content of its own, including articles and opinion columns.

prefers to stick to topics he knows, which in his case is U.S. politics. It is unclear why other conservative Web sites remain unconnected to the international community.

The Conservative Link, with its emphasis on domestic politics, remains a top provider of access to conservative sites in the United States. Unlike other sites, which attempt to provide news, opinion, and columns, Williams simply provides links to as many conservative groups as possible. The result is a well-designed, useful page for other organizations who want links from this site and for users interested in politics to begin their searches. Incidentally, The

Conservative Link provides links to a few sites aimed at liberal politics, which appears to be a growing custom among conservatives on the Web, notably on the Republican National Committee site. There is little evidence that the liberal or progressive sites reciprocate.

A visit to The Conservative Link leads to links to nearly 200 groups interested in conservative politics. These groups range from the Republican Party to the Christian Coalition and include college Republicans, humor and satire sites (including the Washington singing group, the Capitol Steps), and groups such as home schooling organizations that tend to identify with conservative causes. A few of the groups, such as the Western Journalism Center, are professionally run and well-funded, while others, including The Conservative Link itself, are strictly volunteer efforts.

Town Hall is one of the professional conservative groups that is a center for Internet access to users interested in conservative politics. Whereas The Conservative Link provides little except links to conservative groups and causes, Town Hall appears to be a central place for conservative opinion. In addition to links to other groups, Town Hall includes news articles, opinion, and the columns of conservative writers. As is the case with The Conservative Link, however, there is no apparent effort to move beyond domestic politics. What Town Hall does offer is a sort of central browsing site for visitors with conservative interests, and there are links to other groups, especially large mainstream groups, such as Newt Gingrich's Progress & Freedom Foundation. The links are scattered, with some in the margins of the Web page and others forming a list on a separate page.

Unlike The Conservative Link, which is a private effort by a single person, Town Hall is a Washington-based organization supported by the conservative groups that share its pages and by advertising. Town Hall's managers say that the group exists to promote discussion of conservative causes and to provide a basis for issues research. Promoting group interaction and mutual support, rather than just access, is clearly a part of Town Hall's role.

▶ A Turn to the Left

The Web site of the Institute for Global Communications, profiled above, is probably the broadest of the sites on the nets that cater to liberal causes, however it is not the only one. The site that claims that it was first is called Turn Left (http://www.cjnetworks.com/

> The Institute for Global Communications provides links to a vast number of liberal and progressive sites, including many that operate internationally.

~cubsfan/liberal.html), which provides a number of unique resources, as well as links to other groups on the Internet that are trying to provide information to visitors who share a liberal philosophy. Like The Conservative Link, Turn Left is the work of one person, Mike Silverman of Lawrence, Kansas, who runs the site as a hobby. Turn Left is more than just a collection of links to other groups sharing a belief in liberalism. It is also loaded with access to publications, studies, voter information, and opinions. One interesting feature of Turn Left is Silverman's guide to dealing with what is in his view the Republican-controlled media. This section on the site is designed as a tutorial for groups that want to get their views published. One of the things that makes this effort of Turn Left intriguing is that it virtually mirrors equivalent information aimed at conservative groups trying to get information published, despite, in their view, the liberal media.

While Silverman claims that his site is the number one liberal site on the nets, the Institute for Global Communications remains the primary focus for interaction among liberal groups on the nets. In addition to providing a comprehensive set of links to other groups, IGC also provides a collection of five issues-oriented sections that give groups and individuals with specific focuses a place to gather information. The five sections—PeaceNet, EcoNet, Labor-Net, ConflictNet, and WomensNet—divide issues by topics, but also provide links to each other. A group trying to gather information for action or support from another group can find most of what they need on IGC, which is one of the better organized and better managed of the resources for the political left on the nets.

▶ The Nets and Group Interaction

In the old days of politics, meaning before the 1990s, political groups were rarely more than local in scope. In those days, mostly because of the difficulty in communicating with one another, local groups worked essentially alone to see their interests changed into action. Sometimes, either because of a news report or a common connection, a group might find another with a common interest and exchange some help and information, but in general there was little interaction.

While some groups, specifically radical organizations from the far right and the far left, populated private computer bulletin board systems, and a few other technologically advanced groups, such as the space advocates mentioned earlier in this book, managed to build networks based on the nets, there was not much until the Internet started to grow explosively.

Even the commercial on-line services did surprisingly little to en-courage the growth of political activity. This may have been because of the cost of entry, which effectively barred those with limited fi-nancial resources and groups with small memberships. It may also have been due to the methods of allocating space on the computers and that commercial services may have felt that organizations with more potential members would provide a better financial return.

In either case, most of the on-line activity was limited to such major groups as the Republican and Democratic parties, who had lots of members. Even major pressure groups, such as the NRA, had limited success in penetrating the commercial services, which is one reason groups of all sorts gravitated to the Internet when it began to open up to popular use.

Once they were on the Internet, the political groups benefited from two technological advances that permeated the nets shortly after their introduction. The first was the software that created the World Wide Web, which enabled these organizations to encourage their members to go on line even if they were not computer experts. The second innovation, and potentially the more important of the two, was the development of fast and effective indexing tools. While the Internet has had a variety of search and indexing tools for a long time, many of these products were slow (you got a response by e-mail), hard to use (they required a complicated and poorly documented command string), and only had limited effectiveness, so even if you used the search tools correctly, you did not always get the results you wanted.

Once the Web got started, a number of companies started creating effective search engines that looked for a number of characteristics, such as the title of a Web site or its contents. For example, if you wanted to look for the words "progressive" and "politics" throughout the Web, all you had to do was ask. One of the early popular search sites, Yahoo, was critical to the success of many such sites, as is clear from the importance both the Democrats and Republicans attached to making sure their Web sites were listed there as soon as possible.

Once the Web was running and search tools became available, political groups quickly began expanding their operations from simple newsgroup postings and mailing lists to Web sites, and because of the hyperlink capabilities of the Web, these sites also began to link up with other like-minded groups. By late 1996, it was clear that the networks of links between groups was only the beginning and that there is a lot more that groups with mutual interests can do to use the nets as a means of cooperation.

▶ Groping for Groups

Political groups can and do cooperate using the nets as a medium. In many cases, such cooperation takes the form of single-issue organizations that find a philosophical home in a larger group, and, in some cases, these are groups that share some level of common interest.

For example, environmental groups that are working to preserve a specific species or a particular section of rain forest could work closely with an environmental group that has a different agenda (such as outlawing commercial logging on public lands), because the actions of each group could further the actions of the other.

In many cases, such groups would rarely find each other without the nets. With the worldwide communications medium of the Internet and the other on-line services, these groups can now offer moral support, coordinate activities, share logistics, and even cooperate on getting legislation introduced. This ability to have groups function in concert can be very powerful, because until recently it was only the major political parties that were able to wield much clout, and they had a stake in the process. Groups that have been effectively frozen out of the process can now bring considerable force to bear, which can have a significant effect on the political process.

There are a number of activities on the nets that allow groups to work together, and these activities can take place regardless of the physical location of any group, which opens up the international arena to group action. For example:

- **Find other groups with a common interest.** A number of groups in the political arena are interested in environmental issues, taxation, fair elections, the media, education, or the Bill of Rights. While many of these groups may not share the same goals, they can find each other on the nets and share any common interests.

- **Join with other groups for a common goal.** Sometimes it pays for several groups to join together in a single action, whether it means getting a law passed (or killed) or agreeing to participate in a court action. The collection of groups involved in the Internet, civil liberties, and political action that banded together to oppose the Communications Decency Act of 1996 covered the political spectrum, but they coordinated through the Internet to successfully overturn the law in court.

- **Form an alliance to create a larger group.** Many times local groups find that individual action, even by several groups with a common interest, is not effective. In such situations groups can band together to form a larger group or an umbrella organization and advance their agenda by pooling their resources.

- **Foster the development of smaller groups.** A large group, such as a national political party or a large pressure group may often find it difficult to be effective at a local level or in an area where they do not usually operate. These groups can form local groups that draw on the communications medium of the Internet for their information and keep up to date on the issues in ways they could not accomplish alone.

- **Link with equivalent groups.** In some instances, there is not a lot one group can do to work with another, even though they share common ground. In such instances these groups can still communicate ideas, share lessons about how the electorate reacted to proposals, and learn from each other. International connections with other groups are particularly useful in this area, because, while it is difficult for groups from one country to be involved with activities in another, they can still share support and information.

- **Provide mutual alerts.** The speed of the nets is one of its most valuable characteristics. Because communications on the nets take place nearly instantly, an event of interest to a group that takes place in one part of the world can be reported to a group in another almost at once. When groups agree to cooperate by providing alerts of events about which they are concerned, they effectively leverage the members of the other groups into becoming their eyes and ears. As the Prince William County government found out to its dismay, such an alert mechanism can allow a small group like the Piedmont Environmental Council to effectively resist the actions of a government or a major corporation.

In many ways, the activities of the left and the right on the nets are quite similar. While there are differences that reflect the personalities involved and their levels of funding, there is little evidence that the electronic world is the sole purview of one side of the political spectrum or the other. In fact, there are few differences between the means of managing group-to-group links on the nets, but the differences that do exist could be significant. Briefly, they are two. The left seems to be much better connected internationally, and the right seems to have more content on their sites, especially in their focus areas.

International links are extremely rare in activities dominated by the right. Where such links exist, they appear to be incidental, in that the person responsible for the page has a favorite overseas site, but there is little apparent effort to expand the operations of the right beyond the borders of their respective nations. On the other hand, the activities of the right appear to be much more narrowly focused on specific issues important to their members. If a group relates to the media and its alleged liberal bias, then that is what its Web site will contain, and you also will not find items on taxation or environmental issues.

The left, meanwhile, has sites on the nets that abound with international connections. Those sites also typically represent a larger number of groups and have more links to other groups. Therefore, if you are of a liberal mind, you can wander through sites involved with issues of the left, apparently for hours. Many of these sites involve workers committees or environmental groups that are global in nature, while others push issues, such as animal rights, that cross borders. What is more rare is the depth of focus that exists routinely on sites run by the right.

It would appear that the content of the sites on the nets mirrors the approach to politics of the groups involved. Many groups on the right are narrowly focused on issues that they press until they get satisfaction, an area in which the left appears less successful.

Despite the increasing number of Web sites and links, it appears that political group communications on the nets is only now on the road to development. While a number of groups on both sides of the fence do cooperate with others of similar philosophy, most of the cooperation is limited to a Web site link or perhaps a short blurb on a home page. True depth of cooperation has not happened to any great extent and may not for some time.

One reason it may take a while for such cooperation is that this activity is still the purview of only the major political parties. Since these parties are well along in their efforts to take a leadership role on line, much cooperation can flow through the traditional parties, rather than through less formal pathways. If the major parties can provide the resources and the facilities to support issues and groups as they come to them, then they will become a major force in fostering on-line political activity. Otherwise, at least for some functions, the major parties could find their role being challenged by groups that only exist on the nets and that share an electronic cohesiveness rather than a physical existence.

The reason that the existing political structure could find itself challenged is because today's political organizations are organized geographically. While this makes sense from the point of view that elections are conducted geographically, it makes less sense for groups that are trying to mold opinion or apply pressure. As a result, those organizations that work best in the new virtual space of the nets and learn to exist apart from the constraints of geography will find that their use of the new electronic medium is more effective. Ultimately, because they know the new media so well, such groups will be more effective at pursuing their agendas.

If the major parties are to be successful on the nets in the long run, they will have to structure their electronic communications departments so that they are in a position to take advantage of the borderless world of the nets. To some extent, this is already happening, as was shown when the Republican National Committee found Internet users from around the world attempting to join the party. To take advantage of this international reach, however, will require a much broader vision than is currently seen in any of the major political parties.

scape   _ □ ×

dit View Go Bookmarks Options Directory Window Help

        Home   Reload   Open   Print   Find   Stop

Netsite: http://www.democrats.org/

t's New?   What's Cool?   Destinations   Net Search   People   Software

7

N

The Press and
Politics on the Nets

To some, the role of print and broadcast media is ending. There are many who would say that the electronic world is a new medium that is leaving the traditional news media behind because it can deliver exactly what information any person wants. To those people, the model of an information flow that begins at a central point and extends outward to listeners, viewers, and readers who only take in the information is history and the age of the new media is already here.

Perhaps it is, but the fact remains that the vast majority of voters, campaign staff, politicians, and the press are not that deeply immersed in the new media, and for them the traditional media is still where they get the information on which they base such decisions as who to vote for, who to support, and to whom they should donate money. In short, for the political process in the closing years of the twentieth century, the traditional media is still the central source for most information.

Of course, that does not mean the nets—the new media—are not important. In some ways the traditional media can amplify the importance of the nets and the people who use them to affect decision-making. The traditional media, in many cases, get a great deal more information from the nets than most people think. More important, the new media is playing a bigger and greater role every year.

Many people outside the press do not realize the extent to which the traditional media and the new media of the Internet and the commercial on-line services depend on each other. The assumption that they are two different things, that the nets are somehow fundamentally separate from the traditional media, is wrong. In fact, the new and old media have become so closely intertwined that in many ways they are aspects of the same thing.

While the close connection between the new and traditional media should not surprise anyone who has studied them, there appear to be great differences in the perception of each. Whereas most users of the nets know quite well that misinformation abounds and are careful to check before they base a critical decision on information found there, people seem to be more trusting of the traditional media—perhaps because they are more familiar with it—and are less likely to question its information.

In reality, a growing proportion of information found in the traditional media stems directly from the nets. The reasons are many. Newspapers and televisions stations look for information everywhere and take what they can find, but there is more than just the opportunity to find information. It is easier for reporters to find information on the nets than nearly anywhere else. Unlike the way reporters find information when they are searching through courthouse records and police blotters, the nets are well-indexed, retrieval is fast, and the information nestles easily into the confines of their word processors. Combine this with staff, funding, and training cutbacks and workload increases, most reporters take whatever information they can find, do their best to make sure the details are credible, and write their stories.

The result of the pressures on the media and the reporters who work for the media is that political users of the nets form a sort of "back channel" partnership. Political content providers and sources of information create a ready supply of convenient news and feature information about the political process. The members of the media provide a credible channel for the political content providers to get their information to the public, especially the public that is not on line.

There are additional dimensions to this picture. Because on-line users often find political information on their own, and also see it in the papers and on television, they get the same information from multiple outlets, reinforcing its credibility. Handled properly, this reinforcement can take rumor and speculation and give them the impact of fact.

One clear example of the amplification effect of material from the nets being repeated in the news media happened in November 1996, when former White House Press Secretary Pierre Salinger repeated charges of a government cover-up involving the cause of the crash of TWA flight 800. What apparently happened was that Salinger found copies of documents on the Internet that purported to show such a cover-up. These documents, which first appeared on the Internet shortly after the tragedy, became an international news story when Salinger, then a member of the news media himself, provided a wealth of lurid detail. Salinger's assertions died down quickly, however, mainly because so many reporters had already seen these documents when they originally appeared and knew they were false. In fact, the close link between the traditional news media and the nets was clearly shown when news programs and newspaper stories showed pictures of Internet Web browsers with the original copies of Salinger's conspiracy documents. In this instance, information from the nets both created a sensational story and helped kill it.

While the Salinger story was not exactly the sort of event that usually crops up when political organizations and the media come together, it illustrates the effectiveness of the nets in providing the source for news and the ability of news originating on the nets to take on the guise of legitimacy, whether it is true or not. Political organizations that understand this relationship between the news media and the nets can get their stories told very effectively. Likewise, news organizations that understand how to find credible, accurate information on the net and can spot what is suspect, find the new media of the nets to be a nearly limitless resource for information. The nets can in fact be Lisa McCormack's wondrous Library of Alexandria.

▶ The Dynamics of Interaction

Political organizations and the news media conduct a surreal dance in the on-line world. The roles of reporter, news source, writer, and subject change places, sometimes without warning. Some organizations, understanding the dynamic, benefit. Some members of the media and some media organizations also benefit while others are co-opted. This dance can take several forms:

- Planting news
- Spinning news
- Becoming news
- Providing news background
- Providing news sources
- Providing news access
- Providing coverage pressure
- Distributing press releases

Exactly how an organization chooses to mix the news media with the nets depends on the organization and its funding and staffing. While getting on line is not expensive, making a massive commitment to on-line interaction with the media is not cheap. Likewise, some organizations are more likely to use traditional media because they have good access to it, while others will use the Internet because they need its access. Of course, to make this work, organizations need staff who are skilled and managers who will let them use their skills.

▶ Planting News

One favorite means of getting coverage that seems either neutral or even favorable to a cause is to place a provocative document on a site that the group seeking coverage knows is frequently indexed and then just waiting for someone to call.

Tanya Metaksa, executive director of the National Rifle Association Institute for Legislative Action, says that the NRA-ILA has learned to be very effective in making information available and then waiting for the media to discover it. "I figure it helps us with the press immensely that we are putting out credible materials that they can come up and get and use for what ever purpose they have in mind." The key, according to Metaksa, is credibility. While an organization can pick what information they want to make available, the information they provide must be absolutely true and verifiable.

Metaksa is involved in a number of federal and state legislative issues every year, and each of those issues involve the news media. "We strive to be as accurate as possible." Metaksa points out that one reason the news media visit the NRA site on the World Wide Web is that the organization tries hard to make sure that the information available to the media is checked out and accurate. "We are very, very cognitive of our credibility," she explains.

Apparently, the news media is cognitive of the NRA's credibility as well. Stories originally placed in documents on the NRA Web site that subsequently made national news include a letter from House Speaker Newt Gingrich promising support for legislation repealing the ban on assault weapons, a variety of features on women as handgun owners, features on self-defense and self-protection for women, and features on lower crime rates in states that allow citizens to carry concealed weapons. Likewise, the results of an NRA-funded study on race and crime appeared nationally immediately after they were first announced on the NRA Web site.

Many political Web sites go even farther and make the ability to search for information a part of their basic design. For example, when the Web site of Republican presidential candidate Patrick Buchanan went on line, it included its own search facility that would let visitors to the site look for any word or set of words they liked and be taken to the document that contained that information. This meant that members of the news media could always get Buchanan's views on an issue, even if the candidate could not be reached directly or if the campaign staff member responsible for that function was unavailable.

A local search facility, coupled with the power of the public search engines available on the Internet, can help make sure that an organization's views are reflected frequently and accurately. When both the Democratic and Republican national committees went on line with their Web sites, one very high priority was to make sure that the major search sites, notably Yahoo and later AltaVista, listed them as soon as possible.

▶ Spinning News

Like the fax networks of a few years ago, sophisticated political organizations know that reporters check their e-mail often, especially when they are covering major events. Sending spin by e-mail is getting very popular and is very effective.

In January 1996, while President Bill Clinton was delivering his State of the Union Address, Jonathan Knisley and other Republican staffers were hard at work. Soon after the president made each major point in his speech, the GOP staff would post a bulletin to the Internet, with each bulletin including the Republican take on that issue.

At the same time, the Republican Party's Internet staff posted the points to their Web site, but, more important for the moment,

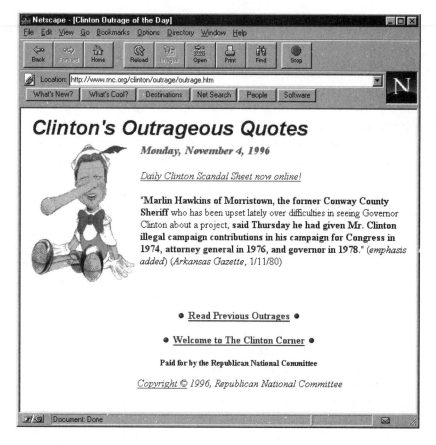

Netscape - [Clinton Outrage of the Day]

File Edit View Go Bookmarks Options Directory Window Help

Back | Forward | Home | Reload | Images | Open | Print | Find | Stop

Location: http://www.rnc.org/clinton/outrage/outrage.htm

What's New? | What's Cool? | Destinations | Net Search | People | Software

Clinton's Outrageous Quotes

Monday, November 4, 1996

Daily Clinton Scandal Sheet now online!

"Marlin Hawkins of Morristown, the former Conway County Sheriff who has been upset lately over difficulties in seeing Governor Clinton about a project, **said Thursday he had given Mr. Clinton illegal campaign contributions in his campaign for Congress in 1974, attorney general in 1976, and governor in 1978.**" (*emphasis added*) (*Arkansas Gazette*, 1/11/80)

● Read Previous Outrages ●

● Welcome to The Clinton Corner ●

Paid for by the Republican National Committee

Copyright © 1996, Republican National Committee

Document: Done

> The efforts of the Republican National Committee to spin President Clinton's quotes in their favor included making them available on the Republican Party Web site.

they sent e-mail to their media list. Many reporters, knowing that this would happen, checked their e-mail repeatedly to keep up with the Republican spin on the issues, and in many cases those e-mailed points made it into the stories being filed about the address. Republican staffers were also able to answer questions and handle requests for interviews. In addition, because reporters knew the Republicans were responding immediately, they were able to craft their stories to reflect this from the start, which helped ensure that the Republican view of the issues was well-represented.

The Democrats have used the same techniques. When Kansas Republican Robert Dole announced that he would retire from the U.S. Senate, within hours the Democratic National Committee sent out a statement to reporters that Dole was abandoning his constituents in his ambition to seek the presidency. This statement was soon followed by others in an e-mailed newsletter called *Demo-cratic News,* which provided short takes on the election, the Republican-controlled Congress, and related issues, such as influence charges aimed at the National Rifle Association.

While the charges against Dole following his announcement did not play well in Washington, other attempts at providing spin via the Internet did. For example, when the Republican majority in Congress scheduled a vote to repeal a recently passed law that outlawed types of firearms labeled "assault weapons," the Democratic National Committee's efforts to deliver political spin by e-mail went into high gear. Reporters and others on the *Democratic News* mailing list were sent updates on the Democratic Party's position. "GOP Lines Up with Terrorists, Gangs, Drug Dealers," read one headline in the March 22, 1996, issue of *Democratic News.* That story was followed by charges that the NRA had essentially bought the vote through millions of dollars in donations and then by a list of recent crimes from around the nation in which police officers were shot by criminals wielding assault weapons.

Of course, not every Democratic effort at spin was used against the Republicans. The Democratic National Committee also used its e-mail access to the press as a way to deliver talking points, announce new features on the DNC Web site, and push their own agenda.

The Republican National Committee used slightly different versions of the same techniques to put the GOP spin on events involving the Democrats. Using e-mail to deliver press releases, statements of position, and responses to coverage in the media, the GOP staffers got their word out both through general releases and targeted mailing lists. One example of a targeted list used by the Republicans was the "Daily Clinton Scandal Sheet," which started up in the last few weeks of the campaign and went exclusively to members of the media. The sheet was an attempt to add fuel to the already touchy issue of President Clinton's ethics and the ethics of his staff and advisers. The RNC also used the scandal sheet to press its points about the events involving everything from Indonesian donations to the Clinton campaign to drug dealers who had their photos taken with the president.

While the RNC also used methods other than e-mail, finds by the party's opposition research staff were funneled directly to the media using the scandal sheet. Those finds included such items as a $325,000 donation to the Clinton campaign by a California businessman that the Republican Party said was being sued by two former employees of a peace foundation headed by the businessman.

The scandal sheet, e-mailed in this case on October 24, 1996, also said that the businessman had sworn in court that he was not a U.S. citizen and was without any assets. As the election drew near, the activities of the scandal sheet grew more intense. In many cases, the fruits of the GOP's research, as reported in the scandal sheet, appeared in the media within days. While it is certain that the scandal sheet was not the only means by which the media learned of alleged misdeeds by the Clinton campaign, it was one of the factors that kept the issue in front of the press.

▶ Becoming News

A number of political sites on the Internet became the subjects of newspaper and television stories on what political organizations were doing on the nets. Information about the latest happenings on the parties and candidates respective Web sites appeared regularly in the e-mailed newsletters from the candidates and the parties. This was done in part to remind reporters to look at the Web sites and in part to encourage reports about the sites. By getting the media to treat the sites as news, the parties and the campaigns were able to get word of their existence out to the public.

The publicity about political Web sites generated immediate activity on those sites. While all of the officials running such sites reported their impressions of heightened activity following stories in the media about their Internet activities, Eric Loeb actually charted it. Loeb, who started keeping track of activity on Senator Ted Kennedy's Web site while he was working for the senator's 1994 re-election campaign and continued to do so afterward, found that the initial story about the site in *The New York Times* generated a flurry of activity from the Senate Democratic Web site. Other events, including an announcement of Web sites for a number of Democratic senators, also generated such activity.

During the 1996 presidential campaign, when Loeb was working as a consultant for Senator John Kerry, he found similar activity. The difference in 1996 was that the Web was much more popular with the media, and, as a result, stories about political Web sites or stories reporting on events concerning the Web sites became frequent additions to the feature sections of many newspapers and favored segments on news shows.

The Washington Post, for example, never let the nets get far from view during the 1996 election season. Such stories were a regular part of that paper's Thursday "Cybersurfing" feature, which included short items on the Web sites of the major political parties, the candidates, and the national conventions. Other features included stories on Robert Dole's announcement of his Internet address at the end of his first debate, along with a screen shot of the Web site posted by a Democratic Party sympathizer that led people to the Clinton-Gore Web site if they made a mistake in typing the name of the Dole site.

Other stories that featured political sites included one by *Post* staff writer Elizabeth Corcoran, who profiled some of the new technology the Democrats used in their convention Web site. An article by Corcoran in the *Post* Style Section (August 29, 1996) described what she called a fresh blend of "quirky insights and technology" in the use of the Java programming language to animate the convention site. Such features were certain to generate traffic for the convention Web site, even if the viewer was merely curious about the technology. Clearly, part of the reason for using such material and making sure it was publicized was to attract the interest of potential voters.

Of course, the *Post* did not wait for the conventions to start writing about political Web sites. Previous coverage included features on early activities and on a Harvard University–based page featuring political third parties. Likewise, *The Washington Post* was by no means the only newspaper covering such activities. Features on political sites ran in papers nationwide and drew interest wherever they appeared.

At one point the Internet itself became a bone of contention between candidates Dole and Clinton. During Clinton's visit to Japan in early April, the staff maintaining the White House Web site placed a link on the site that led to an Internet server supported by the Japanese Foreign Ministry. The server contained a number of documents about the trip that the White House staff apparently felt would be of interest to Internet visitors. Dole blasted the link, suggesting that it meant that the Japanese were "writing trade policy papers for the White House." In reality, of course, the White House staff was simply following a common practice of providing access to related sites—something the Republican National Committee also does when it provides a link to the Democratic National Committee's Web site.

Such stories about Web sites did a great deal to generate interest in political activity on the Internet. Ben Green, a campaign staff member for Massachusetts Senator John Kerry, noted that one of his activities involved collecting information that featured Kerry's Internet activities when such stories ran in papers outside Boston. Green

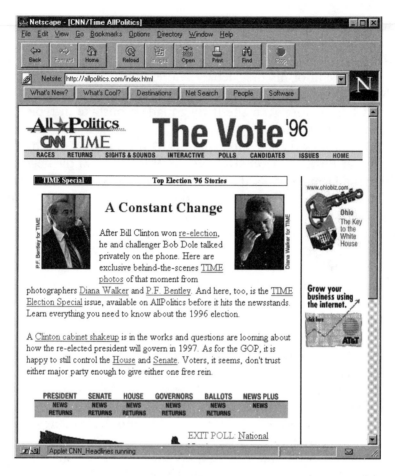

> One press consortium, AllPolitics, presented news gathered by reporters from both Republicans and Democrats on the Web site as a way to provide 1996 election coverage to Internet users, as well as to publicize their more traditional news outlets.

said that such interest in Kerry and the Internet made it much easier to communicate with voters electronically, because they frequently left their e-mail addresses when they visited the Kerry Web site.

While the traditional print media clearly loved stories about the Internet and politics, there was also plenty of activity elsewhere. A number of news organizations created political Web sites of their own. Some, including All Politics (http://www.allpolitics.com), run by Cable News Network (CNN) and *Time* magazine, and Politics Now (http://www.politicsnow.com), served by ABC News, *The Washington Post, National Journal, Los Angeles Times,* and *Newsweek,* were widely used as starting places for members of the media not already working for those outlets.

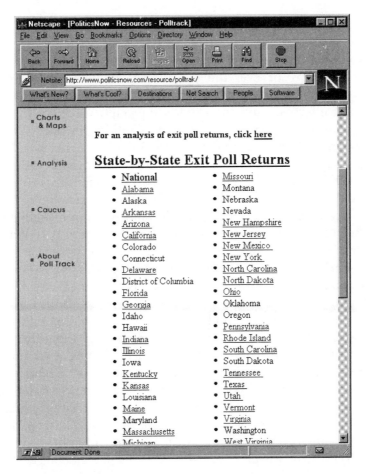

For an analysis of exit poll returns, click here

State-by-State Exit Poll Returns

- National
- Alabama
- Alaska
- Arkansas
- Arizona
- California
- Colorado
- Connecticut
- Delaware
- District of Columbia
- Florida
- Georgia
- Idaho
- Hawaii
- Indiana
- Illinois
- Iowa
- Kentucky
- Kansas
- Louisiana
- Maine
- Maryland
- Massachusetts
- Michigan

- Missouri
- Montana
- Nebraska
- Nevada
- New Hampshire
- New Jersey
- New Mexico
- New York
- North Carolina
- North Dakota
- Ohio
- Oklahoma
- Oregon
- Pennsylvania
- Rhode Island
- South Carolina
- South Dakota
- Tennessee
- Texas
- Utah
- Vermont
- Virginia
- Washington
- West Virginia

> Another organization, Politics Now, provided its services to the users of the Internet, as well as to smaller local news organizations, with up-to-the-minute information, such as detailed state-by-state poll results.

The media-run Internet political outlets worked hard to get the attention of Internet users interested in politics. One reason, of course, was that such activities brought them attention and would expose the public to their more traditional activities. The second was that these sites and others like them provided good ways to get noticed, and quoted, by smaller outlets, and eventually get the attention of their readers.

In effect, the major political journalism organizations had found a way to become news themselves, which meant that not only were the major outlets providing news to Internet users, getting quoted by smaller outlets, and providing a central resource to connected political junkies, they could even report on the existence of these sites and in effect cover themselves and each other.

▶ Providing News Background

While it is not as sexy as some efforts, simply providing on line an electronic copy of everything available, including press releases, platforms, speeches, point papers, and policy initiatives, is one of the most effective ways for a political group to receive coverage in the traditional media. It helps reporters reflect positions accurately and often helps ensure their inclusion in a subsequent story. When a reporter who is short on time begins browsing through the nets, the group will appear, and the information the group wants to see publicized can be incorporated easily into a news story.

Of course, such means of making information available is one of the most common uses of the Internet, America Online, and CompuServe. All of these services have extensive areas that are used by companies, organizations, and other entities, and one of the major uses is providing background. For political groups, such availability can be critical.

Both the Republican and Democratic national committees keep extensive files of their basic information on line, primarily to make that information available to the news media. As Anne Gavin noted, the Republican Party used such information heavily to make up for the fact that the party's convention had its media facilities located inconveniently far from the convention site. This distance made the availability of everything from speech transcripts to the party platform very important to getting adequate—and accurate—coverage.

All of the major presidential candidates made detailed information about their proposals available on their Web sites as well. At both the Dole and Clinton campaign sites, for example, reporters could count on finding the full text of the day's speeches, the most recent press materials, the daily calendar, and the candidate's take on some issues. Many local and statewide candidates had similar pages, and, in fact, the existence of such information is one reason given by some Kerry voters for their support in the 1996 senatorial race in Massachusetts.

▶ Providing News Sources

Not everything goes out over the World Wide Web. For example, if you want your executive director to appear on the morning news, getting a few quotes on the nets, along with an e-mail address, phone number, and other contact information can help, especially if his or her comments are germane to whatever is the hot topic of the

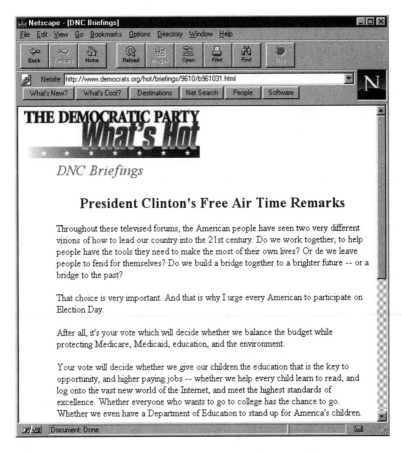

> Political parties used the Internet heavily to get unfiltered information to users and news organizations. Such background information included press releases, the text of remarks and press conference responses, and even complete transcripts of speeches.

day. During the 1996 elections, both major parties and many smaller participants sent members of the media frequent updates of who in their organization was available for comment, who had something to say, and whom to contact to arrange an interview. Late in the 1996 presidential campaign, reporters could count on statements by Republican Party Chairman Haley Barbour several times a week, usually accompanied by additional information about how to get more details. This availability of comments meant that the Republican viewpoint remained in front of the members of the press, despite what had become a general belief by then that their presidential candidate was not going to win.

In many cases, the information made available to the media is less dramatic. The Republican National Committee, for example, makes it a point to make the e-mail addresses and phone numbers of its officials available to the press. This information can be found on the Internet, and it is also available through the organization's mailing lists. Many pressure groups do the same. The idea is that if you make it as easy as possible for reporters to locate the officials that your organization wants quoted, the organization's views are more likely to be heard.

An example is the e-mail activity of an environmental group called the New West Network. This group, which has the stated goals of promoting the economy and environment of the West and encouraging political candidates that agree with the group, is headed by Brad Udall, son of former Arizona Representative Morris Udall. Brad Udall started sending out information that made it clear how to find out more about the group, how to contact him for comments, and how to get involved with the group through the Internet. Despite the appearance of a large, well-organized group, the New West Network was actually made up entirely of Udall. While he freely admits to his role as backer, leader, and complete membership, his ability to get attention for his group shows how effective even small groups can be in using the Internet to make their voices heard. In Udall's case, by the time he surfaced nationally in May 1996, his organization's budget was around $5,000, at least according to the claims he made in his e-mail communications and press releases.

▶ Providing News Access

Ultimately, being available and ready to provide good quotes and good copy helps ensure coverage for a group. Providing access information through e-mail to the news media and making sure they know that they can call at any hour of the day or night will help spread the word. While the press always appreciates knowing how to get in touch with the leadership of an organization, sometimes all that is necessary is how to reach the person that can deliver an important piece of information quickly. In those instances the nets are invaluable. In fact, many reporters would prefer having more than anything else the pager number or car phone number of a reliable press contact that can deliver useful information than nearly anything else.

While the provision of information about how to find news is closely related to the provision of news source information, there is a difference. Information about access means that a reporter has on hand the detailed information about where to look when they need something in a hurry, where to call when they need something sent to them, and where to page when they need an urgent response.

Such news access information is already commonplace for reporters outside of politics, especially in the business press, where corporate public relations consultants routinely provide key reporters with everything from their private office numbers to their home phone numbers to ensure that they are available when the press needs them. Likewise, corporate press relations managers make sure that members of the media have information ahead of time about where they can locate corporate information, including financial statements, biographies, operational details, and the like, and they update these lists frequently.

The practices of corporate public relations started to make their way onto the political scene in 1996, when public relations officials from the political parties and candidate staffs started to provide periodic e-mail updates of contact information to the press. This included, among other information, the personal e-mail addresses of key campaign officials—the ones officials checked themselves rather than the public e-mail addresses that were checked by staffers most of the time.

▶ Providing Coverage Pressure

For groups that cannot get the desired press coverage, there is another option—pressure through e-mail. Groups on the nets find that they can use their e-mail connections to get their members to call or write specific people in the media or specific media outlets often enough that it creates enough interest for a reporter to write a story.

If you cannot get your story told in the press, you can put your position on the Web (or on Usenet if you cannot afford a Web site) and then get your members to call the targeted media with questions about the position. Eventually someone will go to the nets looking for details, and your group may get the attention it wants.

E-mail, of course, can work two ways. As the NRA's Tanya Metaksa pointed out, organizations can be very effective when they use their own e-mail lists to notify members that the organization wants them to do something. This is especially useful if an organization wants a news organization to cover them or their participation in an event. The idea is to get members to react with both e-mail messages and written mail to convince a news outlet that their coverage is inadequate or inaccurate.

To a limited extent the efforts of Senator John Kerry's campaign to provide enthusiastic crowds for media consumption were similar to this. When the campaign sent out e-mail to thousands of supporters asking that they appear at an October rally hosted by an environmental group, it was not the environmental group that campaign staffers wanted to impress. Instead, the idea was to make the senator look strong and, as a result, to convince the media that his campaign was not stalled. It worked.

▶ Distributing Press Releases

E-mailing press releases to targeted reporters may sound very traditional but it is extremely effective. Those messages do not get delayed in the mail room, lost in the fax pile, or buried on the desk. Instead, they give the reporter an edge of an hour or two, and maybe a day or two, and they help ensure that the organization's word gets out accurately, because the release language can be moved directly into the reporter's word processor.

While most reporters will claim that they hate press releases, the fact is that they depend on them heavily for a variety of uses. Even though press releases are rarely exciting, they are official positions and information from the organization sending them out, and they frequently provide useful information. The problem is that there are so many of them that many reporters simply lose the information they contain, even if it is something they need.

When political organizations send out electronic press releases, they help ensure that their releases will not end up unopened and in the trash. Likewise, reporters often retain electronic releases on their computers, because the information in them can later be retrieved easily. For example, if a reporter gets a release on campaign scheduling, it is fairly simple to locate the schedule a few days later by using the simple search capabilities of most e-mail applications. A paper release would almost certainly be in the trash by then, unless it contained information so vital that it was filed, and then there was the prospect of it not being found.

▶ Becoming Part of the Game

The 1996 election season encouraged another change in the manner in which the press covers elections—from objective observer to active participant in the process. While the major news organizations did not actually take sides any more than they usually do, they did become much more closely connected with the process than in previous years. This connection came as a result of the new on-line political news sites run by traditional media.

The two major sites, All Politics and Politics Now, are funded by consortia of news organizations. They exist primarily as extensions of their parent companies, specifically as ways to leverage the news already gathered and to present that news to a more varied audience. In addition to gathering and reporting news, however, the media political news Web sites also provide links to the Web sites of the political parties about which they write their news stories.

While merely providing a connection to a site does not imply endorsement, there is always the question of how the sites are chosen, who chooses which sites to make available, and how many political entities are linked. To date, neither All Politics or Politics Now has made any effort to explain the selection of political sites to which they link. To their credit, both organizations appear to have made a credible attempt to cover even minor candidates who qualified to run in the 1996 presidential election. All Politics even listed every presidential candidate who qualified with the Federal Election Commission.

In more localized races, it is not always clear that the media is objective or that objectivity is always possible. In the 1996 Massachusetts Senate race, for example, the *Boston Globe*'s Web site (http://www.boston.com), wrote about and linked to Senator John Kerry's rapidly growing and well-designed Web site. While there was plenty of coverage for challenger William Weld, there was no coverage of his site because he did not establish one until near the end of the campaign.

This difference in campaign tactics also meant that when Internet users were reading about the Massachusetts campaign, they could link to Kerry's Web site for more information and had to be content with the information about Weld provided by the *Boston Globe*. Because the Weld campaign did not have a site to which to provide a link, should it have been the newspaper's responsibility to provide at least basic background information on Weld? Or, because the Weld campaign chose not to have a Web site for most of the campaign, was that simply a missed opportunity by the Weld campaign?

Not knowing the answer to the previous questions in this instance only means that, for now, there is no sure answer. As with other sorts of political coverage, mixing the Internet and the on-line services into the equation makes the issue more complicated, but it does not change the basic nature of journalistic responsibility. News organizations have the responsibility to cover the news but not the responsibility to make the news themselves.

On the other hand, journalistic standards do apply in covering politics in the electronic media as in other areas of coverage. When a newspaper or television news show asks a candidate or political organization a question but does not receive a response, they usually say that the question was asked and report why the respondent said they would not or could not answer. This is why you see comments in print to the effect that an official was unavailable or on travel, that their lawyers said they could not comment on a pending action, or some such indication that the question was at least asked.

Stories about political activities on the nets may not appear as balanced as other political news stories, especially in areas where the new media of the nets is still a novelty. Whether it is print, broadcast, or on-line reporting, much coverage seems to be one-sided (regardless of the side at a given moment). The story is presented, the Internet address or URL (Uniform Resource Locator) is given, or, if the story is on line, the link is provided, and there is no mention of what is going on in the rest of the race.

In a political story, news outlets will not tolerate the appearance of bias and at least refer to what the other side is doing, even if they were doing nothing. This should also be the case on line. Thus, if a newspaper's Internet page were doing a story on a candidate's Web page, the other candidate could also be mentioned, a link provided, and the page could lead to either a page that simply says, "Senator Jones has not provided an Internet address for this link" or lead to the candidate's Web page. That, at least, makes it clear that a link was offered but that the campaign and not the newspaper failed to provide the information.

Part of the problem may be that the nets are a new medium, known better to reporters than to editors. As a result, reporters know how to find information and how to leverage the nets to yield information quickly and effectively. The editors benefit, because such activities can cut staff hours dramatically, but they do not realize that the information such efforts provide is not necessarily accurate or complete. Therefore, the information found on-line must be confirmed in much the same way that any other source of information is confirmed by a reporter. Just as you cannot trust a drug dealer or town gossip to provide more than a tip or a rumor, much of the information on the nets is provided by people and organizations that have more in mind than just passing along information.

One suggestion for editors is that they treat information found on the nets with considerable suspicion, at least until verification by an external source. One primary reason for doing so is that it is not always clear who is responsible for material on the nets, and while the information may be accurate, there is no certain way to be sure. Even sites on the nets run by supposedly reliable organizations can find the information they provide changed or altered in some way, as managers of the Web site belonging to the U.S. Department of Justice found in 1996, when vandals substituted images provided by the department with pornographic photos.

There are a number of guidelines that make sense when using material from a news source that depends on the nets, whether it is for compilation into a news story or for information gained while reading such a story. Here are a few:

- Is the Internet site the only source for the information? Without some corroboration, there is simply no way to know for sure that the information, regardless of how official it looks, is true. Remember, even experienced journalists and White House officials, such as Pierre Salinger, can be fooled.

- If there is another source, is it also on the nets? Again, there is no way to know who is actually providing the information you see, and the same person can supply information for multiple sites. Creating two seemingly unrelated sites with provocative information is an excellent way to snare unsuspecting reporters.

- Is the report balanced? If you are writing about activity on the nets by one political party, candidate, or movement, are you including the others involved in the same issue to the same extent you would if it were a traditional news story about traditional politics? Writing a glowing story about one party's Web site while ignoring the other is just as biased as writing glowingly about one candidate's positions or their campaign literature.

- If the story provides a link to one individual or organization, does it provide links to the others? Even if the link leads to a page with a statement saying there is no page to link to or a statement from the party or candidate saying their page is still being developed, links are a means of access that should be unbiased.

- If the story is to appear on line, do the links lead to equivalent pages, and are there an equivalent number of links to candidate or party Web sites? For example, if one link to the Democratic candidate leads to the page for the party platform, is that also where the link will lead to the Republican candidate?

- Is the story linking use of the nets to overall political quality? Not all candidates are well enough funded for elaborate Web sites. While this may not be the case for presidential candidates of the national parties, it can be an issue in smaller races. Is the article about Web sites suggesting, even indirectly, that the quality of the candidate's ideas or positions is somehow based on the quality of the candidate's Web site or the lack of a site? If so, this could indicate a bias by a reporter that is comfortable with technology and can afford it, versus a candidate that cannot or who feels that the money would be better spent on other things.

The combination of politics, the nets, and the media can be very powerful. The media are probably more capable than the population at large in ferreting out available on-line details and are probably more accustomed to using computer-based research. Thus, using the media as a form of surrogate Web surfer can make sense.

Unfortunately, it also means that with less direct control over the source of information, it is possible to be taken in by information that is simply not true. While the problem with false information is a problem everywhere, reporters and their audiences have learned to filter out obviously bogus information from the traditional media. With the nets, those skills are often less well developed. The lack of a filtering skill when it comes to the nets means that it is possible to see a document on line and use it, when no reporter would be fooled by the same document if he or she were to run across it in a government file or be handed the document on the street. While this problem will eventually be solved as the on-line world becomes more a part of everyday life, for now, it is a risk. Editors and readers need to be suspicious of material from the nets unless they know there is another confirming source.

The need for a confirming source also provides a challenge for organizations that would use the nets to reach the media. It is important that the nets are not the only means of access. Political organizations need to make sure they also provide access that involves real people, real voices, and real experiences. While not all of the media will demand such access, the reporters that care about completeness and accuracy will. The real challenge of the nets will be to find a way to provide both the information needed by the press and the access the press needs to make sure the information is true.

scape

dit View Go Bookmarks Options Directory Window Help

Home   Reload   Open   Print   Find   Stop

Website: http://www.democrats.org/

at's New? What's Cool? Destinations Net Search People Software

Growth
of Cyberspace
in Politics

"When I first came to the Congress in January of '93, it was virtually a desert here that had not been cultivated yet," says Anna Eshoo, Democratic representative from California's Fourteenth District. Eshoo has been a leader in encouraging the introduction of technology into the operations of Congress. The reason nothing was being done, Eshoo says, is that the members were simply uninformed about what the nets and technology could do for them. "Most members didn't know anything about the technology, it simply was not in use and I don't think it was on members' lists of things to do to make sure that it would be part of their office and their constituent services and operations."

Now that Representative Eshoo has been working on finding new ways to use communications technology to improve access for her constituents, things are changing, although slowly. While she has been one of the leaders, Eshoo has not been alone in trying to move Congress and the U.S. government further into the age of the nets. There are, however, many roadblocks to change, and they must be overcome one at a time.

As Eshoo mentioned, some of the roadblocks to change in government are because of a lack of knowledge. Lawmakers frequently come from nontechnical backgrounds, their careers are devoted to making governmental processes function rather than dealing with such things as the Internet, and many of them attended school decades before they achieved high office. Thus, it is not surprising that they do not have a handle on why the nets are important or how the existence of the nets (or other technology for that matter) can affect the way legislation is created or laws are applied.

One journalist who covers Congress reported during the passage of the Telecommunications Act of 1996, which included the language of the previously proposed Communications Decency Act, that the senators who wrote the bill had never even used a computer, much less had access to the Internet or even e-mail. If that is indeed the case, it is no wonder that the act failed to address the Internet as it actually is or, for that matter, the reality of modern communications.

This great gap in knowledge may not be surprising, but it dramatically affects the way in which lawmakers accept such things as the nets in both a legal sense and a practical sense. Adding to the confusion in government, there are a number of legal obstacles to providing access to government services and functions through electronic communications. While many of those legal obstacles can be overcome, either by appropriate design or by recasting the law to allow such things, they are still roadblocks to progress and efficiency.

Perhaps the greatest block is the question of constituency. Each member of the House of Representatives is elected to represent a single congressional district. Each senator is elected to represent a single state. While members of Congress may occasionally oblige citizens from outside their districts or states, their primary role is to serve the people who elected them. In order to do that, they must be sure who they are dealing with and be certain that the person actually resides in the area they represent. When they are contacted by organizations, members of Congress must make sure that the groups are what they claim to be and that the groups actually represent their stated interests.

It is not particularly difficult to pretend to be someone else when using e-mail, nor is it difficult for an organization to claim to be something it is not. For these reasons, representatives and senators have tended to insist on written communications, physical locations, and some means to make sure that they are dealing with a genuine person or organization. Confirming the identification of a person or group can be difficult on the nets, because one of its greatest strengths is to reach across borders transparently and gather information anonymously.

▶ The Silicon Valley Challenge

It was into a formidable collection of obstacles that Anna Eshoo decided to lead her effort to modernize at least her office, if not all of Congress. Eshoo had some benefit in the fact that she can run her office however she wants. "In terms of the staff and the operations," Eshoo explains, "we are solely in charge of our own office operations and the constituents that we serve. This [computer communications] is now looked to not only as a technology but a technology that has a sense of familiarity, its members [her computer-savvy constituents] have a sense of familiarity with it and that it can heighten and improve communications with your constituents." Eshoo says that part of the reason she feels members of Congress need better communications with their constituents has a lot to do with the size of their jobs. "Each one of us is responsible for 575,000 people. That's no small problem to be able to communicate effectively with them. So, I think it's on the move. Has everyone embraced this technology? No. Does every member of Congress understand it? No. But neither do all of the American people."

Fortunately, here Eshoo has an edge. "I have represented this district where this technology was born—and not only born, but raised and then given to the country and the world." Eshoo says, describing the district that she represents near Palo Alto, California. "So I have a sophisticated constituency, and these technologies and the use of them are embraced throughout the district. And yes, there are some wealthy areas of the district, but wealth is not the deciding factor. It's more state of mind."

Getting the right state of mind can be a problem. While the use of computers and the nets is growing rapidly throughout the United States, the growth has been uneven. While technology has penetrated deeply in areas near Silicon Valley in California, as well as near Boston and Washington, D.C., there are many places in the country where the penetration is much less. On the other hand, the growth of technology is pervasive throughout the country, and it will eventually exist in all areas.

The right state of mind depends on more than just constituents who know about the nets and the technology required to use them. It also requires that legislators at all levels, including Congress and the state legislatures, the bureaucracies and the local governments, realize exactly what communications technology will do for them and for government.

▶ Electronic Democracy

"The Kennedy School, which has always thought of itself as an institution that trains leaders in government, felt that leaders weren't focusing on technology issues, that historically they had basically delegated those to somebody else," says Dr. Jerry Mechling, director of strategic computing and telecommunications in the public sector at the John F. Kennedy School of Government at Harvard University in Cambridge, Massachusetts. Mechling also directs the Kennedy School's Electronic Democracy Project, which is an attempt to teach government leaders what technology can do to make government more efficient, more responsive, and less expensive.

A great deal of the work that Mechling and others pursue involves making use of the nets as a way to deliver services to people. Delivery of services is currently one of the hottest areas of interest in government, because it is an area in which improvements are noticed immediately, and it is something that governments have not accomplished as well as most people think they should. For these reasons, service delivery gets a lot of interest in Dr. Mechling's projects.

"What people are actually doing with technology that they turn to us for advice about is simply using the networks that are now forming as distribution channels for public services, information-only services, or transactional services," Mechling explains, describing how governments are showing interest in using the nets. "You can reach them over the Internet, you can reach them over the 1-800 services in conjunction with computer networks. You know, the fax-based services."

Mechling also says that much depends on rethinking how and where the actual transaction between the government and a citizen takes place. "A whole variety of things that are moving the service transaction from face to face with the government official. There's some network-mediated operation, and why we find that so interesting, besides the fact that people are doing that a lot, is it offers a pretty high benefit to citizens in terms of convenience." Mechling explains that basing government operations on delivery through a network can benefit all sides.

"They can reach things twenty-four hours a day without having a major trip to stand in line in a government office, but there is also personalization. They can basically look at more information before they decide what to do and they can reduce the unit cost. When you can take over time services that used to require face-to-face meetings and allow them to be handled remotely, you can set up those remote offices in less costly settings. You can organize them differently. So, remote service is more efficient, but when you can move it to self service and have citizens wield their own as it were, that's a big hit for efficiency."

While there is a lot to be said for the immediate gratification of solutions that use existing networks and bring obvious results to citizens, Mechling says that there is really much more important work to be done. One reason why government does not work particularly well now and it costs so much to provide government services is that the government does not work at the same level of efficiency as the private sector, in part because it has not had to do so in the past and because the lack of efficiency is due to a lack of understanding of technology and communications.

"Technology was thought as something that you use to automate or improve just a little bit what was already in place," Mechling says, explaining the dimensions of the limits of understanding, "but there were increasing numbers of examples, largely out of the private sector initially, of people conceptualizing what a service was, how it reached its clientele, or how it was produced. But to be successful with those more radical changes, more reengineering-like changes, more strategic changes, to do that well, you had to handle the political problems of getting people to agree to deal with the discomfort of going from here to there organizationally, and that required political leadership and required a much better partnership between the technology community and the political civil service."

One of the goals of the Kennedy School's Strategic Computing Project is to help form partnerships between the private sector, especially the technology community, and the government. Mechling's Electronic Democracy Project includes such a demonstration effort in its work with the IBM Corporation in Washington, D.C., where IBM has built a laboratory that lawmakers and government officials can visit to see technology in use, solving government needs. Significantly, the IBM effort includes more than just federal applications, because the goals of the Electronic Democracy Project include state and local government efficiency as well as efficiency on the national level.

▶ Solving the Constituency Problem

Efficiency, however, is not the only problem, and neither is familiarity with technology. Government officials must be sure that services are being delivered to the people who are qualified to receive them but are denied to those who should not get such services. Services that use delivery means such as the nets, which can originate from anywhere, have a particularly difficult task of delivering services correctly. The process of proving qualification must be sufficiently strict that the government officials delivering services can retain their financial accountability, while not inconveniencing the citizenry to the extent that they object to the network service delivery.

The extent to which a person must prove themselves to the government depends to a considerable extent on what service is being delivered. For example, the Internal Revenue Service, which delivers tax forms and instructions over the Internet, does so freely. That agency does not care who gets a tax form and is concerned instead with making sure that every form is available as fast as possible to every taxpayer.

On the other hand, such organizations as the Department of Veterans Affairs or the Social Security Administration must make certain that they are delivering checks to the people who are supposed to receive them and that medical benefits are going to people who are actually veterans or old enough to receive Medicare. Because these government agencies are involved in the delivery of money and valuable services, they are open to fraudulent claims. Therefore, such agencies need a way to make sure that the person requesting a service is properly identified as well as qualified.

Confirming identification and qualification over the nets (or even over the telephone) is difficult. While this may change when technology that supports Smart Cards (devices about the size of a credit card that contain vast quantities of information) becomes available in the United States, it will still probably be a while before you can receive your Social Security check from a kiosk in a shopping mall.

Work on solutions to the questions of constituency and qualification, however, is taking place. Here, too, Representative Eshoo has taken the lead by introducing the first e-mail service aimed specifically at serving her constituents. First, however, she had to deal with the existing House e-mail system. "The e-mail system here as it was set up in the House of Representative is less than efficient. You think of e-mail as being something that is going to short-circuit the U.S. Postal Service by days, weeks, plus all the hours left over after that. And the truth be known, it's not so terrific. I mean it just gives snail mail a new meaning," as Eshoo describes one of many reasons why the Congress is not doing all that well communicating with constituents by e-mail. "There were even some messages that were lost, that wouldn't come to the office."

"I think that communication with your constituents is probably one of the most important functions of a representative," Eshoo continues. "So I think that [a new, constituent-oriented mail system is] going to accomplish a couple of things. First of all, it's far more efficient and effective. I think that confidentiality plays a part in this as well, which helps us, in that if it were not the case, we might skip over many steps. So someone comes in, establishes the mail box that then becomes part of our database, and we can get back to them because it comes right into our office."

Eshoo says that her new constituent mail system, which is tied to her Web page on the Internet, allows constituents to register, confirm with their names and addresses and contact information that they really are who they claim to be, and then be able to communicate with Eshoo or her staff. With this system, Eshoo knows with whom she is dealing and whether they are constituents. Eshoo points out some of the distinct advantages over the old mail system: "It's not going into some central system in the bowels of this building somewhere and wait for that to be distributed to us." She adds that the new system should make things easier for the people in her district. "So, I think that it is wonderful constituent service, but it also demonstrates, because we put out a message to the Internet Caucus and other interested senators and members of the House about this so they could call into our office, use this as a laboratory, come and see how it works, so they could learn and then duplicate that, take it to their offices as well."

Eshoo feels that once service initiatives become available that use technology and the communications potential of the nets, people will begin to find ways to use their new access to the government to improve their lives. She also thinks such a change will help people revise the way they think about government, much in the same way that some companies in the private sector have earned reputations for caring about customers. "I don't think Nordstrom [the Seattle department store chain famous for service] would have the reputation that it does were it not for the fact that they go more than the extra mile in terms of customer service," Eshoo explains, drawing on the concept of citizens as customers of the government. "I'm a daughter of a small businessman, and my dad always said that we're here to serve our customers, to do everything we possibly can to take good care of them. Otherwise, he was a jeweler and watchmaker by trade, [and] he said there are other jewelry stores, people can go elsewhere to buy these products."

While she realizes that a citizen cannot go to another government, the principle still holds. "Well, in many ways they can't necessarily go to other places for the kind of information they may need from us, but I do think that the federal government overall certainly doesn't enjoy a warm reputation with an awful lot of people in the country. They don't think of it as personal service, they don't think of it as efficient, and they don't think of it as effective."

Eshoo believes that the ability to deliver services and information quickly and easily will do a lot to make people more satisfied with the government, while at the same time making the government more efficient and less wasteful.

▶ Finding the Keys to Efficiency

"The early step that the people are taking is merely using the networks as a delivery channel," Jerry Mechling explains as the beginning of making government more efficient by use of the nets and other related technology. "And that's attractive because it is an early benefit that people notice—convenience and better service—but there is not huge disruption in the producing organization, so you can do it this year as opposed to four years from now."

Unfortunately, there is a limited amount of improvement that can be done simply by moving delivery to the nets. There must also be fundamental change in the way government views technology as a means of producing and delivering services. Mechling says that to get greater change into an organization, especially a government bureaucracy, one of the first things that must be accomplished is to help people understand how this will affect their jobs and careers and get them to adopt technology despite those changes.

"When you get the more fundament change in the production side," Mechling explains, "when you're telling people, 'no, your job isn't this, it's completely different; no, your managerial hierarchy in your career steps aren't what you thought they were, they're completely different,'" then adopting technology, regardless of how it is delivered, becomes a much greater problem.

Because the job is so difficult, and Mechling notes that it is much harder in government than in the private sector to make such fundamental changes in an organization, it is proceeding very slowly. He believes that eventually the government will understand that a number of processes must be reengineered, but he does not think it is going to happen soon. For now, he says, most of the changes depend on the nets, on communications, and on related technologies that improve delivery of services to citizens. "But what we've done, in my view, is to change the channel," Mechling says. "We've electronically distributed an increasingly important array of government transactions, information-based and other. We got a huge row to hoe yet there, but then we'll also come on to the big 'let's change the way it's produced' and that's just starting."

The problem, of course, is that the government, especially the bureaucracy, is not in a big hurry to change. For the moment, better delivery systems are seen by many as a way to keep the taxpayers satisfied that improvements are on the way. Mechling does not think the situation will last forever, however. Instead, he believes external forces caused by changes in the electorate over time will eventually force the governments into making basic changes.

"[It will take] credible pressure over time," Mechling says, pointing out the factors that will eventually change the way government functions. "Policy involvement. I mean it's being driven by the tax revolt. We want government to do more with less, and we see how other institutions respond to that outrageous demand and make it work. So, we want our government to do it too, and as long as people keep at that, if there is tenacity, there will ultimately be progress."

Despite the fact that Mechling believes the bureaucracy will eventually yield to the pressure to improve efficiency, he does not think it will be easy. In fact, Mechling thinks it will require some significant intervention on the part of the government's leadership to make such a change work. "There are great difficulties here in the structural problems of cutting back on total resources while also investing in experimental ways of delivery sources that in the long term are necessary for efficiency improvements. I mean, there is a great move to squeeze the government, but as you squeeze the government, the constituencies that are getting squeezed wake up, come in, look over your shoulder, and scream, 'Don't squeeze me!,'" Mechling says, explaining the problems with battling constituencies that frequently stall attempts to reduce the size of government. "And, so, from the government side, either as a politician in an oversight role in a legislature, state, local, or federal, or the leaders of government agencies, they find it very hard to rub two nickels together for the experimental attempt to do something different. That's a horrible problem for us to try to solve. And I don't see systemic ways to easily solve the problem. I see that there are certain places where sort of the forces come together, where you get an executive leader and enough running room with the legislatures to do important things."

▶ Doing Important Things

Of course, planning and stating needs is one thing; actually using the reins of government to make changes is something else entirely.

Representative Anna Eshoo thinks that Congress is already beginning to change, both in the way the institution uses the nets and in the way it responds to others who use this new form of communications. "There are far more offices on the Hill, both on the Senate side and the House side that have actually installed technology in their office, who have e-mail, that have Web pages, and so that's all for the better," Eshoo says. "Now, our constituents are communicating with us more through this medium, and other offices are." Eshoo also takes issue with those who would say that Internet-based communications are ignored by Congress. "Of course there are many manifestations of it, many uses, and while there are some that believe that organizing around legislative issues by the Internet is something that members don't pay attention to, "I don't think that there is anything that takes the place of substance in terms of the message. So that is always part of the burden, the responsibility of the com-

municator. So I disagree with that because we pay attention to it."
Eshoo notes, however, that e-mailed junk mail is no more effective
with Congress than any other sort of mass mailing. "If you get 2,000
messages that are exactly the same, then it's the same as a postcard
campaign."

Former White House staffer Jock Gill thinks that the government needs to do a lot more than simply replace traditional means
of interacting with voters if the government, and the country, is
going to remain a solid force into the next century. According to
Gill, the need for change requires new ideas and new approaches, in
much the same way suggested by Jerry Mechling. Gill says, "If you
look at evolution, one of the interesting things that you want to
have is the largest possible idea space, and you want to be able to
support it as rapidly as possible. Because if you limit your idea
space, you limit the probability you'll find a successful strategy,"

He notes that part of what is going to drive the government into
using what the "new media" of the nets is the growing competition
with other economies and other countries. "Just look at the economic change in terms of scale and scope of the U.S. economy, the
importance of the U.S. dollar, the fact that we are no longer the
largest trading unit. Look at the great themes of the spring of '96, of
uncertainty in the workforce, anxiety about the future, which didn't
exist in the 1950s. Well, how do we respond to that politically? I
don't have the exact answer for that, but clearly, we have to, if we
want to evolve successfully," Gill adds, pointing out that in may
ways the United States is being forced to keep up with everyone else.
"As rapidly changing as the world is, we'd better make sure we max-
imize our idea space by maximizing the diversity of the voices heard,
and diversity in participation, rather than minimize it."

Gill says that the need to promote evolution in the way the government functions and in the way it uses the new media means that
the government and the politicians that run it must find ways to
make change happen, even if it is painful. Gill also points out that it
is important to decide what the goals of government and the goals
of any changes should be. "If we don't ask the question 'What sort
of America do we want to build in 2025?' it's very hard to imagine
how we could optimize the system because we don't know where
we are trying to go."

Gill says that much of what the government needs to accomplish in his view could be done by simply making more information
available to voters everywhere and by accepting input from voters

electronically. While he admits that such a process could require significant changes to the way the government does business, he thinks that, in the long run, it is necessary. "How do we put time and substance back into the deliberative process, into the dialogue of what kind of country we want to have, into the nature of the regulatory process?" Gill asks. "Right now, for example, if the regulatory regime is part of the restraint system that we have to optimize, what is the regulatory process?"

Gill says that the current regulatory process is unnecessarily complex. The complexities include the requirement that comments be made in writing and cannot be submitted electronically. Likewise, any public comments must be viewed in person at the library of the agency concerned with a proposed action of the government. Despite the fact that the technology that would allow citizens to make comments electronically and view comments and proposed actions of regulatory agencies exists today over the Internet, it is not used. Instead, everything takes place at a location set aside by the agency, to which interested parties, or their lawyers, must travel.

So, how do you get to Jock Gill's vision of a radically changed government from one that is only now beginning to understand electronic mail? There are a number of steps involved, but two of those—getting acceptance by the people who work for the government and getting the new ideas paid for—are probably the most difficult. In Jerry Mechling's mind, these two steps go hand in hand.

"If there is a single problem that has to be solved, again and again, that maybe people aren't talking about as much, it's the analogy in the public sector to what is venture capital in the private sector. Bill Gates destroyed IBM and brought a new set of activities into being, not by getting IBM senior managers to allocate a little bit more to new ways of doing business, but because there was a venture capital market that funded new ideas so that when they grew, they could attack the old ideas and force that kind of change." Mechling says that the availability of some force analogous to venture capital could make a big difference in the way individual agencies cope with changes.

"In the public sector, it is very hard to get venture capital," Mechling says, "and I think it's a problem that has to be solved. I'm attracted to some of the ideas in the federal government. They are trying to get the Cross Agency Investment Fund by raking a little money off of FTS2000 [the federal government's communications initiative] to create a fund that would do this sort of thing. I see rolling funds for this sort of new capital investment. I see capital budgets used to fund technology investments in state and local governments, and to amortize them over a number of years. I see user charges to turn to as a new way to fund these new things, but the tax base is a very hard source of funding for new things when it's under such attack as it is."

With a form of venture capital to help create the new technology initiatives and new interest in finding new ways to incorporate communications technology into a new form of government operations, Mechling believes that the acceptance for such initiatives is already underway. While he notes that there will always be some resistance, he says that such resistance is likely to fade as more and more people familiar with technology, with working on the nets and in a connected environment, enter government. "Politicians come from society," Mechling says. "This society is inundated now in an idea that we are part of an information age, things are changing. You can't read through a magazine, look at any nightly TV without being barraged with the fact that there are new things afoot and technology is right in the center of it. Well, people are getting to like that," Mechling continues, "from constituencies, and people are coming through careers that expose them to these ideas before they become politicians."

Mechling emphasizes that "even lawyers are now noting that the legal profession has got to adapt to information management being more powerful. You know, information is a cheaper commodity than it use to be and they have got to address this. So, over time," Mechling predicts, "with the new folks, the younger folks, consistently saying, 'Why hasn't the government done these things? We've got to get the government to do these things,' I see momentum being built that is a resource to tap into."

Mechling also says that part of the problem with the resource is that it is not spread broadly enough. He believes that will change but not without additional problems. One of the problems is making sure that you get what he calls the considered opinion of people involved with the process, while at the same time making the process available to a great breadth of people.

Making the problem more complex, Mechling says that any tool that increases power, including access to the nets, is first owned by the powerful. He notes that such technologies as computers and the Internet started out as government-owned resources and only filtered down to industry and then private individuals when the cost of ownership dropped to the point where individuals could afford a computer or pay for access to the Internet.

Mechling says he has initial information from his research that this process of technology diffusion is taking place now with the Internet, as it already has with the commercial on-line services. "The powerful will get initially more powerful, but when the technology at its unit level is inexpensive it will diffuse out," Mechling says, explaining his preliminary findings. "I believe there is a diffusion process, so that the equilibrium issue is going to not be elitist in its impact."

"I may even at some level worry that we want to construct a conversation that taps into people's considered opinion, not just what most is at the top of their heads," Mechling says and points out that there are concerns about the way in which new technology, such as the instant communications of the nets, is adopted. "I think networks will allow people to participate more easily in the 'what's off the top of my head' phenomena. We may have to worry about how we also deepen that which traditionally has been a role for the elite."

"The elite had the time, the energy, and the education to represent all of us who think deeply about problems, and as long as we didn't walk too far away from what we felt, we kept them in check," Mechling says. "A society needs representative democracy, not just lowest common denominator, 'off the top of my head' stuff. . . . Do I think technology is going to increase elitism? No. It may in the short term, but long term it will spread the conversation," Mechling says, adding, "I think there is a need to think about how we make that conversation deep as well as broad."

Anna Eshoo agrees with Mechling that the reach of technology will be very good for democracy in the long run. In fact, when she was asked how access to the direct electronic communications provided by the nets will effect how people interact with the government and their representatives, Eshoo was enthusiastic. "I think it's nothing but good news," she said, clearly excited by the prospects. "I think it broadens it. I think it heightens it. I think it deepens it. I think it brings in a great deal more participation of young people."

Eshoo noted she feels that encouraging participation by young people is critical for the future of democracy. "If young people do not develop a pattern of participation and voting early on, if they don't start that early on in life, many, many studies show that people don't click on and become engaged later on in midlife. So, I think with all of the information that's out there, that especially young people can take advantage of the fact that it will lessen an individual's vulnerability, as it were, to political manipulations that are, in many ways, the dumbing down of America." Eshoo says, "The better informed an individual is, the better educated, and it's not just an institutional education that, as important as that is, but educated in the broadest, fullest sense of the word, the better off we are in this country. That's why I find it so exciting."

"What I find to be the most provocative about all of this is that I think it is great news for democracy," Eshoo says, explaining her enthusiasm. "I can't think of a better time for these two issues to be coming together. The moving into a new century and these technologies that are moving us are kind of the magic carpet that is sweeping us into the next century, and they do converge, they come together, and I think that this is one of the more exciting events for democracy. So I think it's terrific. I can't tell you how excited I get when I think about it. If one really cares about this country, the statistics that would worry one the most are the number of people that don't participate in the political process." Eshoo says that access to the nets and to the government and its representatives should go a long way in involving people in the political process early in life and encouraging them to continue.

▶ Getting from Here to There

There seems to be general agreement that, one way or another, the government will be forced to move into being more accessible and more responsive to voters through the use of technology. For now, at least, that accessibility will be through the nets, especially the Internet, because it is already there. Eventually, however, a wealth of options may emerge.

The factors that prevent an orderly move to a more technologically oriented means of providing services and accessibility appears to be a lack of understanding and interest on the part of the government, both among elected officials and the bureaucracy. That must change as the populace becomes more and more accustomed to communicating electronically and, in turn, becomes less and less patient with officials who will not. The resulting demands for a technology-based service will eventually overcome resistance based on both funding issues and constituency issues. Quite simply, when the voters refuse to stand for such resistance, the government will be forced to find a way.

The real question is whether the government can be made to move without being forced. Again, the general agreement is that it may be. As Dr. Mechling points out, elected officials come from the general population, and when the population expects to use rapid, network-based communications for everyday use, so will the people elected from that population. As the growth of the nets becomes more pervasive, the growth of acceptance of them as a form of communication will become much more broad.

By becoming more broad, democracy will also become more accessible. More people will be able to participate, and as more people are able to participate, the democracy will be more representative of them. By providing easy and quick access to the government, its leaders, and its services, the nets will make the democracy more democratic, and the representatives more representative of their constituents than ever before.

Of course, there are always down sides. The representatives must be sure that decisions are based on considered opinion, rather than whim, but this has been a problem since overnight polling began, and politicians long ago learned about polls. While there are a few down sides, there are many more positive factors. In short, broadening the base of democracy will be a direct effect of opening electronic communications for the delivery of services and for the reception of interest and opinion. Either way, the nets are helping the people take more of a role in their government and that is the function of a democracy.

*E*ffects of Politics

on Cyberspace

In late winter of 1995, ministers from the seven most economically powerful countries in the world, the Group of Seven (G7), met in Brussels to discuss what was being called the "information society" by the Europeans. During the meetings, one theme stood out above all others, both in the level of concern and the amount of attention it was given, as compared to issues that seemed more pressing to some, such as guaranteed access to communications. The theme of the meeting was a question: How to protect European society against the onslaught of American culture as the Internet and other on-line services catch on?

This question and related others that were raised at the meeting continued to haunt relations among the G7 nations. Would Europe have any way to protect itself against American culture on the nets? Would Europe be able to ensure European content in material that was available to European users? Would European governments have control over the nature of material they found offensive?

Some of these questions were answered in less than a year. The state prosecutor's office of Bavaria forced CompuServe to shut off worldwide customer access to a handful of newsgroups, charging that those newsgroups, because of their names, were suspected of containing objectionable material. While the prosecutor's office had not actually checked out those groups and there had been no complaints, CompuServe shut them off anyway, despite the fact that several were innocent of any objectionable material and a few actually contained information designed to help improve the lives of severely handicapped people. The issue raised by the German prosecutor's office was that the newsgroups in question contained material that if minors had access to them violated German law. Some of the material was not suitable for minors, because a few of the newsgroups contained pornographic images. On the other hand, many of the groups contained no images or other objectionable information. In any case, CompuServe kept those groups closed until the service was able to change its software so that it restricted users with German addresses.

Another problem that later drew consternation to the Internet was when members of the French government suggested that Internet communications should be kept out of France unless the material was in the French language. In December 1996, the French group "Defense of the French Language" sued Georgia Tech over its English-only site on the Internet. The group, which serves as the French language police, says that the law in France requires all such sites to be in French in addition to their language of origin. The Georgia Tech site in question is based in Metz, which is the seat of the university's European operations. The suit was expected to go to trial in January 1997.

While all of this was going on, the government of China started licensing Internet users and began construction on a national filtering system that would allow the Chinese government to keep out any material, including political and economic news, that the Chinese government did not want its people to see.

Back in Europe, the European Commission began to study in spring 1996 a proposal to require cyberspace material to have at least 51 percent European content if it was to be seen in Europe, in much the same way that European broadcasting rules require television stations to carry program material that is at least 51 percent European.

While the debate on European content was progressing, the U.S. government was in court fighting a challenge to a law that would prevent the Internet from carrying "offensive" material. While the U.S. government was under an injunction that prevented enforcement of the law, federal law enforcement agencies continued to collect information on alleged violators of the offensive materials law, on the chance that the government would prevail and immediate enforcement would be needed.

In the case of the U.S. law, it is instructive to note that if the provisions were to be followed, many of the government's own documents and some of its Supreme Court decisions would be prohibited from public access on the Internet, because they meet the law's definition of "offensive." While the challenge continues at press time, the U.S. provisions are only a small part of the attempts to control the nets worldwide.

All of these examples illustrate that the real question is not whether there will be government and political control of the nets, but rather how much, what kind, where, and how pervasive. One way or another, politicians will attempt to gain some control over a medium that many view as out of control. The only matter for debate is what the nets will look like once things calm down.

Professor David Farber, one of the founders of the Internet and Moore Professor of Telecommunications at the University of Pennsylvania, does not think things will change much, at least not right away. "The Communications Decency Act [CDA] will not go away," Farber predicts. According to him, the federal government will try to find a way to move past the CDA. "They will try to find a constitutionally defensible position to restrict the things they object to on the Internet," Farber says, predicting future federal actions. He also believes that the U.S. government will try to find ways to let the states impose stricter standards on the Internet. Farber refers to a similar situation in Australia, where individual states have laws that prohibit people from saying certain things about politicians. Because the Australian laws vary state by state, Farber suggests that the current trend there is to adopt the strictest law in any state as the standard for the Internet in Australia.

Pointing to recent U.S. cases in which a bulletin board operator in California was prosecuted for violating obscenity laws in Tennessee (because bulletin board system users in Tennessee could dial in through the Internet and use the BBS), Farber believes that as a result the nets will become subject to the strictest interpretation of any law in any community.

While it is still too early to tell exactly what sort of regulation may be implemented by the federal or state governments in the United States or what they will be allowed by the courts to implement, it is clear that the nets are already being affected by attempts by service operators to make sure they do not take a chance at pushing their luck anywhere.

For example, as mentioned earlier, in 1996 a local prosecutor's office in Bavaria, Germany, approached CompuServe with a complaint about the fact that the service was making several Internet newsgroups available about which the office had questions. CompuServe responded by blocking access to those newsgroups for all subscribers, regardless of their origin, worldwide. After a few weeks, CompuServe programmers were able to adjust the system's software so that only subscribers entering the system from Germany would be blocked, but for a period of several weeks, CompuServe users worldwide were prevented from using information for which they were paying, at the behest of a single local government.

America Online managed a similar action without even waiting for government action. That service, fearing questions about possible objectionable material on its service, began programming the system so that users could not use certain specific words in public areas. One of those words was "breast." While it is possible that this may have prevented some users from making off-color jokes, it provided a source of considerable consternation for users of that service's breast cancer support group.

Some types of potential regulation are still speculative. There is an urban legend that circulates through the Internet newsgroups about once a year to the effect that Congress is about to enact a "modem tax." This alleged tax, which varies in some details every year, would essentially allow phone companies to charge extra fees for lines that people use with their modems. Each time the legend surfaces, users write thousands of letters to Congress, and then the scare goes away.

The problem with the modem tax scare is that while it is an urban legend, it is not one that is completely fabricated. Such fees have been discussed and could be permitted. In fact, there is no reason these fees would require congressional action, because presumably the Federal Communications Commission and state regulatory commissions could take this action themselves. Whether such a tax would have much effect on either controlling use or regulating users is pure speculation, however, because there is no way to know what form it might take, if it actually comes into existence.

▶ The Encryption Issue

Few attempts to control the way information is handled on the nets raise as much fuss as attempts by federal law enforcement agencies to control the way on-line users handle encryption of their e-mail and other information. This situation is compounded by the fact that a number of software packages exist on the nets that allow users to protect information by encryption methods that are virtually unbreakable with most current technology. Because of this, the Federal Bureau of Investigation and the National Security Agency have been pressing the administration and Congress hard for laws that would require a form of encryption to which the government would hold the key, meaning that a law enforcement agency could read encrypted information. While the proposed laws would place the key in the hands of a third party under escrow, many users believe that law enforcement would not let that stand in the way of their reading e-mail. In December 1996, however, the government's efforts to control encryption suffered a big loss when a federal judge in San Francisco held that many of the existing laws controlling the use of encryption and encryption algorithms were unconstitutional restrictions on the First Amendment.

What's next? Farber thinks that Congress will press for changes in copyright and liability laws so that Internet providers will be held accountable if they are used as pathways when users violate intellectual property laws. Currently, Internet providers are viewed as common carriers of information, much like the phone company. For this reason, they are not considered responsible for the information users move across their systems, in much the same way that the phone company is not responsible for the content of your telephone conversations with someone else. The idea is that a service cannot be responsible for content it cannot control.

According to Farber, a change in the liability laws could change the presumption that Internet service providers are common carriers. At that point, the process of policing content of communications would move from the federal government to the individual businesses providing Internet access, who would try to avoid civil liability. "This would change the net dramatically," Farber says.

▶ The Limits of Understanding

"How do you judge this new medium and what it means?," asks MIT researcher Mark Bonchek, pointing out that one significant challenge to dealing with legislation involving the nets is to understand the basic concepts about what the legislation is intended to regulate. "Senator Exon, for example, had never even used a computer, though he wrote the Communications Decency Act legislation," Bonchek points out. The lack of familiarity with the nets and the people who use them heavily has a great deal to do with the regulatory impact of government on them. For example, the proposal in the European Commission to apply current European mass-media standards to the Internet and to transnational on-line services would require 51 percent of the program material on such nets be European in origin, as is the case with the content of European television. The French have a similar requirement for their film industry.

This requirement shows a fundamental lack of understanding of cyberspace as a medium. As Bonchek would say, it applies a broadcast model to a medium that is not a broadcast medium. The difference is, also according to Bonchek, that broadcast media (which in his definition includes both electronic media, such as television and radio, and newspapers and magazines) operate as one-to-many media, in which one outlet sends information to many recipients. He points out that the printing press worked this way, as do radio and television. This model allows easy definition of what constitutes program material, and it makes regulation of the material easy to define. The problem is that the nets do not work that way.

"Here is a completely different medium," Bonchek says. "It's not a one-to-many medium. It's many to many." Bonchek's point is that attempting to place a broadcast media model over a fundamentally different kind of medium will only mean that the assumptions are wrong and that the model does not fit. This in turn means that impossible demands will be placed on the medium. The European Commission's demand for 51 percent European program content is a clear example—how does the commission plan to define content? If it defines content as Web sites, does it plan to block access by Europeans to Web sites outside Europe once users attempt to access more than a certain number of them? If so, which sites? How would they be limited? Clearly, a familiarity with the reality of the Web and the nets would have shown the European Commission that such a requirement is not only unworkable but impossible to define and implement.

The problem is, unfortunately, that potential regulators continue to misunderstand the nets, and worse, they allow their lack of understanding to color their attempts to gather the control they believe the nets require. In part this lack of understanding is encouraged by the fact that some of the diverse groups that populate the net are well outside the bounds of traditional politics. "The net is a marvelous organizing tool for radical groups that may not like the traditional political process," Farber points out, adding, "If Lenin had the net, it would have taken much less time to have a revolution."

Of course, the nets are hardly the private playground of radical groups. In fact, many mainstream political groups use them to good effect as organizing tools and as one means of getting the word out to a choice demographic group. There is, however, a difference in perception between the politicians who make the laws and regulations and the political professionals who use the nets. Because it is the politicians that make the laws and staffers with limited experience that draft them, the resulting regulations often exhibit a lack of understanding and, as a consequence, attempt to control the medium inappropriately.

The gaps of understanding take several interrelated forms, and while not every law has all characteristics and not every lawmaker is uninformed, the trend has been clear to date. More important, the trend appears to be location independent, meaning that the nets are as misunderstood in Singapore as they are in the United States, Europe, and Australia. As a result, regulators are finding themselves in a quagmire of misunderstanding that results in ill-fitting laws and regulations. The gaps include:

- **Lack of experience.** For many legislators and administrators, the nets are a phenomenon that has appeared suddenly and in a form they do not understand, because in many cases they have never even used a computer or learned to type, much less traded messages by e-mail. To many of these people, even voice mail and telephone answering machines are new technologies of questionable value.

- **Lack of reference.** For users who started using the Internet in college, the concept of cyberspace makes perfect sense, but it is a concept without reference to people who have never used America Online or who have never even seen a computer bulletin board system session in operation. Trying to understand the concept of cyberspace by those without a frame of reference may be like trying to explain a third dimension to a two-dimensional being.

- **Exposure to invalid information.** Compounding the problem is the fact that in every political arena, there are a number of competing forces, and frequently those forces have opposing agendas. For example, in 1995, an antipornography group used a study conducted by graduate student Martin Rimm at Carnegie-Mellon University that purported to show vast penetration of pornography and sexually oriented material on the Internet. Even though Rimm's study was quickly discredited and the university subsequently apologized for it, and even though Rimm eventually admitted that he had done his study under contract for a pornography vendor as an attempt to show a lucrative market, those forces continued to use the study to prove their point. Many legislators were never told that the study was invalid, and few asked their staffs to confirm the validity of the information.

- **Exposure to hype.** Even when lawmakers are not being given false information, they are exposed to hype about the nets from a variety of sources that tend to accentuate the trivial and trendy, while ignoring the parts of the nets where actual work takes place and where important dialogue and research takes place. For example, newspaper and magazine stories about the Internet tend to feature commercial, advertising-related sites, as do references to the Web that appear in television commercials. Because advertising agencies have been quick to grasp the demographics of Internet users and because setting up a Web site is relatively inexpensive, electronic "brochures" on the nets have multiplied dramatically. With them have multiplied Web site addresses that appear in ads, giving many political leaders the view that the nets are little more than high-tech advertising, devoid of a meaningful application.

- **Concern about the population of the nets.** Because the nets are such an effective organizing tool for groups of any size, even small and nontraditional groups can have a powerful voice. Once lawmakers begin to understand that some of the groups they hear from consist of only a few people bound together by e-mail, they then begin to believe that the nets are populated by fringe groups. When they are exposed to flame wars, intolerant exchanges, and irrational attacks that sometimes happen on the nets, those beliefs may be reinforced.

Because of the combination of misunderstanding, misinformation, and concern about potential use, it is not surprising that legislators are dubious about the nets. Couple that with a belief that there is little of value on the nets beyond advertising, and it is understandable that legislators may believe that a broadcast model is as good as any other and that strict regulation is necessary. In fact, most users of the nets themselves are not so much opposed to regulation as they are opposed to inappropriate regulation that ignores the reality of how the nets work and instead attempt to impose a structure that does not fit.

▶ Models for Political Control

At this point in the life of the nets, at least, governments appear to be looking at the nets as a form of broadcast media that is effective at the transmission of ideas but is difficult to manage because it has so many different entry points. This, of course, is to be expected because of its many-to-many method of transferring information, which means that information can enter a country through any Internet or service user that chooses to look for such information. Because there is no single point of broadcast and each user chooses the path through which information will flow to them, real control can resemble an attempt to plug a leaky dike with fingers, except that the many-to-many existence of the net means that a nearly infinite number of fingers would be required.

▶ The Prevention Model

While there are vast differences in the way their governments work, as well as in the economic health of their economies, the governments of Singapore and China share a similar distrust of information from outside their borders. In the case of Singapore, the distrust appears to be mostly oriented toward information that the government feels is either morally objectionable or that criticizes the government. In China, the view of the government appears to be that virtually all information from the outside world is suspect, including political and economic news and information the government considers morally objectionable.

The solution to the dilemma in both countries is to restrict information from the nets before their citizens can see it. In the case of China, this means that the country is requiring Internet users to register with the government and that all Internet access must go through a sort of government-sponsored firewall (a firewall is a means of controlling information from the outside, although it is normally used by corporations rather than countries). Before information will be allowed through for public access, the Chinese government will confirm that it contains nothing objectionable. In 1996 the Chinese government announced that it would require that both individual users as well as foreign corporations use the same standards, meaning that banks and businesses based in the United States, Europe, and elsewhere will be required to filter their business and economic news through Chinese authorities, as will U.S.-based financial and news services, such as Dow Jones and the Associated Press. In Singapore, the situation is much more relaxed and primarily requires local Internet providers to meet government requirements in terms of the information they carry. These requirements, however, are backed up by stiff penalties if providers do not toe the line.

In both countries the idea is to intercept objectionable information before it becomes available to citizens. While in general this model can work, given enough time and effort and sufficient commitment on the part of the government, it ignores the fact that access to the nets does not have to take place through a local Internet provider or a local access number to an on-line service. In fact, one contributing factor to the success of the dissidents during the 1989 Tiananmen Square uprising in China was access to outside communications. Then, the access was primarily through fax machine connections, but those same phone lines can work just as well for reaching the Internet.

In either case, this is the most extreme version of governmental and political control over the nets. The reason is that both governments (and others that will attempt to carry out similar policies) are blocking information for political considerations. Rather than trying to make sure that a specific view is provided but is not blocking other views, the approach in China and Singapore is to prevent users from seeing any view except the one officially sanctioned by the government.

▶ The Ethnic Insurance Model

During a television program in which she shared the podium with the author, Professor Shalini Venturelli from the American University School of International Service in Washington, D.C., pointed out that many societies believe that citizens have a right to receive specific types of information. Depending on the society, this may mean cultural information specific to a group of people or a nation, or it may mean information provided by the government to its citizens. In her studies, Dr. Venturelli found that the basic views of how society interacts with what she refers to as the global broadband network can vary considerably.

During the appearance on the United States Information Agency (USIA) WorldNet television show, for example, a number of callers asked about what they saw as threats to their culture from the Internet. The threats were not perceived as moral or political issues so much as they were concerns that their culture might be diluted by the lure of outside ways. According to Dr. Venturelli, the view of the nets in society helps explain why the Europeans talk about an "information society" while Americans refer to an "information highway."

As a result of this view in which the information environment that society uses is considered part of the overall fabric of society, governments feel that citizens should have access to cultural and political information that reflects the society of which they are a part. In Europe, for example, this leads to demands that a certain percentage of content be European in origin. The issue is not as much commercial as it is based in the roots of the information society concept, that is, that the information content of the nets needs to provide the cultural information to which the citizens have a right. The percentage requirement is there to ensure that those rights can be fully exercised.

While the goals of the European Commission, when it approached content requirements, were more related to ensuring that the right to specific information was preserved than to some sort of protectionism, it is no more workable because it ignores the basic many-to-many nature of the nets. On the other hand, because of the openness of the nets, the European Community has an almost un-limited opportunity to make cultural information available to the entire planet. While it might be impossible to measure quantity, it is certainly possible to ensure that every cultural interest is preserved, provided the budget exists to support it.

▶ The Individual Rights Model

In many nations, including the United States, political speech as well as most other types of speech and writing, is protected by law. Except under specific circumstances, such as national security or (sometimes) public safety, the government is prohibited from limit-ing what people may say or write. While the government may ex-tract penalties for some types of speech or writing after it has been published or verbalized, prevention is prohibited by law. Therefore, the U.S. government cannot place limits on written material, includ-ing material that appears on the nets for purely cultural or political reasons. While there are limits to commercial speech and writing in-tended to protect commerce, even in those instances most speech cannot be prohibited but rather is subject to sanctions after the fact.

The result of the legal protection model is that users on the nets in the United States are protected from interference by the govern-ment in most types of speech or writing. If the government wants to make information available to its citizens, it may, but there is no re-quirement that they use it or even have access to it. In fact, there are limits on exactly what information the government can provide to its citizens, which is why the USIA WorldNet program can be viewed only *outside* the United States. Officially it is government-sponsored information and as such cannot be broadcast to U.S. citi-zens because of laws designed to prevent dissemination of propa-ganda by the government.

The U.S. Individual Rights Model is designed to protect citizens from the government rather than to ensure that any specific infor-mation reaches the citizens. Similar to it are the less formal models in countries such as Russia and other parts of the former Soviet Union, in which the government is so overburdened by funding basic services that there is effectively no control over the nets at all. While in these areas there is no specific protection from government interference, there is little if any capability from the government to interfere. While it could be argued that those countries and societies follow a fourth model, the reality is that they follow no model at all, and as the conditions within them stabilize, one of the three primary models may emerge.

▶ The Political Response

The nature of the political response to the nets will vary according to several factors. The first is based on the perception of the nets by the political leadership. In circumstances in which the political leadership sees a threat either to its power, political stability, or control, the response will continue to be repressive, as is now the case in China. This response provides stability by denying information to the populace, but that stability could be short-term. Eventually, information will leak in, despite the best efforts of the government, if for no other reason than it is impossible to completely close all means of entry to information.

As the Chinese government found out in 1989, some access is necessary to conduct commerce, and if that access exists, unregulated information will flow through it. While the Chinese attempts to stifle information will certainly slow the flow, information is sufficiently intangible that it is impossible to prevent such flow. In addition, the current government of China cannot survive forever, based as it is on the control of a few rulers, many of whom are nearing the end of their lifespans. When they go, the chaos that has pervaded many previous transitions in China will make information restrictions even less likely to remain.

Preserving ethnic interests while allowing a free flow of information is ultimately a more stable environment than the repressive model above. While it is unlikely that the European Commission will ever be able to realize its stated goal of 51 percent European content, it is likely that Europe will be entirely able to present as much cultural information as desired by the government and the political leadership. Making information available on the nets is both easy and inexpensive, and Europe has enough in resources to support such an effort. It likely will have the support of its populace to provide access to culturally important information, as long as all sides get their say.

Unfortunately, not every culturally sensitive society has the resources of Europe. Those that do, including much of Asia and the Middle East, will also be able to ensure that their ethnic voice is heard. Other nations, despite the fact that becoming an information provider on the nets is within their grasp will not. Part of the reason involves a political will to support ethnic groups that may be out of favor, but other reasons include the simple lack of infrastructure to support connectivity to the nets, regardless of political will.

The lack of infrastructure can be crippling. For example, when the Vatican Library and IBM began working on digitizing many of the priceless documents in the library, the original proposal sought to have much of the work done in Argentina, where eventually there would be a major repository. What prevented that was the lack of bandwidth between South America and Europe. The available 56-kilobyte-per-second digital line was simply too slow to support the transfer of images in the size needed for the digital reproductions of the Vatican's documents. Similar restrictions affect many countries, and, ultimately, they limit the ability of their societies to be heard on the nets.

The Individual Freedom Model in the United States and similar models in other locations is not a process designed for stability as much as it is designed as a protection for the citizens against the government. As such, it forms more of an ebb and flow of opinion coupled with areas of relative stability. This dynamic environment ensures that all opinions can be placed in the marketplace of ideas, but it also means that there is no guarantee that anyone is buying.

The political response to this seemingly ungoverned area of information flow will be a continuing effort to govern, at least to some extent. Eventually, because of the way that U.S. law functions, there will be enough case law from Supreme Court actions that the limits of government involvement will become clear. Until then, the political response will be characterized by efforts to take control of some specific area of the nets, followed by a subsequent appeal to a higher authority. The exact response will depend heavily on which political party occupies the White House and Congress and will probably go through several perturbations before practical guidelines are agreed upon.

Ultimately, because of the fundamental differences between the manner in which the nets handle information and the way in which traditional media transfer information, regulation will be limited by practical considerations. In other words, most societies will regulate information to the extent that they can or to the extent that their laws allow regulation, and they will then simply ignore the remainder. While a number of attempts are currently being made in the

United States and elsewhere to criminalize specific types of information transfer, such attempts will be limited in their effectiveness because of the fact that information does not respect borders.

The lack of respect for borders, as well as practical limits on authority, mean that political control of the nets can only go so far before the nets and the people that use them find ways to avoid the control. For example, if restrictions on sexually explicit images become too onerous, operators of systems that wish to carry such images will simply place them outside the boundaries of the country with the restrictions. Because information will reach the desired users in any case, governments will be required to adopt an untenable position of attempting to monitor the private conduct of every citizen who uses the nets, or it will require the politically more expedient solution of deciding to ignore what cannot be changed.

Adding to this growing acceptance will be the growing number of citizens who are part of the nets. In turn, there will be a growing number who realize what cyberspace really is, instead of what the lobbyists and pressure groups say it is. This growth, which will become part of the political process almost immediately, will mean that the nets and politics will become irretrievably intertwined. Outside of the repressive societies, politics and the nets will become one, and as a result it will look a lot like society because it will be part of society.

View Go Bookmarks Options Directory Window Help

Home   Reload   Open   Print   Find

Website: http://www.democrats.org/

News   What's Cool?   Destinations   Net Search   People

10

*F*uture of Politics
on the Nets

"In the not too distant future, I see no reason why the net won't be as effective as television and radio and potentially the press," predicts Professor David Farber, who has been closely involved with a variety of political efforts involving the Internet over the years, helping a number of parties and causes. He also says that he feels confident the new media of the Internet and the other commercial on-line services will be as critical to successful political activity as the traditional media is now. Farber's views are shared by every other observer of the nets and politics interviewed for this book, and while a few declined to predict exactly what form the future would take, there was unanimity in the belief that politics could no more exist apart from the nets than it could exist without printing presses or television.

In fact, the existence of the nets promises to do a great deal to open the political landscape to many more political parties and to groups that might form to address single issues or join to affect specific events. The reason, of course, is that the nets drop the price of entry onto the national stage to a level that nearly anyone can afford. More important, the nature of the nets is such that content matters more than form and substance more than flash. As a result, organizations with issues that resonate with voters stand to gain a great deal from access to the nets, while groups with less popular stands may suffer from the exposure.

In fact, as the nets become more accessible to the bulk of the population, the way in which politics is conducted stands to be profoundly changed. For years, the American political scene has been dominated by the party organizations, with the result that much of local (and thus eventually national) politics was ultimately under the control of precinct officials. It was they who decided the fate of the parties and the candidates they backed, and it was they, in the long run, who made policy and politics.

"We have spent the last twenty years destroying the political party as we knew it," explains Jerry Pournelle. According to Pournelle, the changes in politics were already underway when the nets arrived to provide another medium for activity and in the process began filling a growing vacuum. "When I was in graduate school in political science, you could truthfully say that the real governing of the United States was done by about thirty to forty thousand self-selected precinct committee people who essentially ran the party. And they were self-selected in the sense that almost anybody who wanted to work hard could become a fairly hefty party official, and in those days, the party official had a good bit to say about platforms and candidates and who was going to be the candidate of the party."

Pournelle continued, "Nowadays, primaries are about the only way you get delegates to the national convention. It's pretty well decided, which means the national convention is a coronation, not an actual attempt to select the party's candidate. As we go into more of this electronic communications and the rest of it, I presume that trend will be exaggerated." Pournelle also says he believes that the trend to conducting politics on line could lead to moves toward a direct democracy, rather than the representative democracy that today governs the United States and other Western democracies. The trend worries Pournelle. "I don't know a single political theorist who ever thought that was a good idea."

Pournelle's concerns about direct democracy echo those of many other people involved in politics on the nets. The problem with rapid, often ill-considered, political action, they feel, is that it can lead to government by whim. A single rumor on the Web, a sensational news story, or a well-organized campaign of misinformation might create a sweeping demand to do something that could turn out to be wrong but be difficult or impossible to change.

▶ The Role of Content

While many believe that the nets will grow rapidly in status with regard to political operations, there is less agreement as to exactly how political organizations will use this new medium. Will political use remain as it is now, sort of a combination between printed campaign literature and television ads, or will it become something else? While it is impossible to predict with certainty exactly how the future will turn out, there are already indications. Mostly, they boil down to content and speed. Of the two, content may be the most difficult for those used to creating commercials and scripting events to grasp.

The most important differences between the media of the nets and the traditional media of television, newspapers, and the like is that they are, in MIT researcher Mark Bonchek's vision, broadcast and the nets are not. Instead, when someone looks for information on the nets, they are seeking answers to specific questions or information about specific topics. This difference is critical. If a person wants information about a candidate's position on abortion, for example, that person can search political sites on the Internet, key on the word "abortion," and get just that information. With such a search, it is easy to see which candidates agree with a specific view and, perhaps more important, which candidates have specific views but are trying to avoid the issue. This difference also means that voters can go straight to the issues and bypass the hype and bluster of traditional campaign rhetoric and the spin of the campaign consultants and instead stick to the issues that matter to them.

Of course, there is more to content than just an index of issues. For example, indications are that the Republican National Committee site on the World Wide Web was extremely popular with voters during the 1996 presidential campaign because of the content it provided, including such things as a forum in which visitors to the Web site could express their views on the election or related items and do so with the knowledge that others would see their comments and that the Republican Party leadership would also see them. Because the Republicans did not censor any comments at all (except for a couple of egregious messages that were filled with profanity), the perception was one of a free exchange of information—something that has always been popular on the Internet and which fit in well on this site.

Likewise, the Republican National Committee's use of its Guest Book as an open forum for comments became an important source of content for this Internet site. Even though the Guest Book on the site consisted mostly of the names and initial impressions of thousands of first-time visitors, it was clearly popular reading, perhaps because it was unusual in being openly available, and perhaps because, like the forums on the site, it was uncensored. Comments in the Guest Book entries show the positive impact on visitors who had clearly grown tired of Web sites that were nothing more than brochureware. The GOP offered interactivity during 1996 to a level not previously seen in political sites on the nets.

Of course, the level of interactivity did not help the Republicans win the presidential election in 1996, but that does not mean the Web site failed in its mission. If you read the thoughts of Lisa McCormack, it is clear that the mission of the GOP Internet effort is really looking far beyond the 1996 elections. The Republican National Committee Web site is an effort to gain the attention of frequent users of the World Wide Web over a long period of time. Ultimately, by always being available, by always having useful content, and by always providing an interactive source for information and discourse, the goal is to make sure that Internet users think about the Republican Party when they think about politics.

While the Democratic National Committee began to move in much the same direction following the 1996 elections, the approach during the election season was much more campaign-oriented. If you stopped by the DNC Web site, you were greeted by a considerable effort to convince you to vote Democratic during that election. Any long-term effort had to wait until after the election.

Which approach will likely work better? As is always the case in things involving technology and communications, the answer is a firm "it depends."

The goal of the national parties is twofold. One is to win elections, the other is to increase their numbers. The DNC in 1996 oriented itself toward winning elections, the RNC toward convincing more Internet users to become Republicans. Considering the nature of the nets, it is impossible to say conclusively which approach is the better one, but rather to say that if used properly, both work.

For example, during interviews conducted for this book, Lisa McCormack noted that the Republican Party was working toward a long-term goal of becoming the dominant party in American politics. Even during interviews conducted in the late spring of 1996—well before the national conventions—she was already looking at elections in 1998, 2000, and beyond. She pointed out that the GOP was making significant inroads in the numbers of local and state officials who ran in their elections as Republicans. She also noted that in many states the balance of power had already shifted in state legislatures, county governments, and city councils. Ultimately, these local and statewide offices generate the candidates that run for the House of Representatives, the Senate, and for the presidency of the United States.

This supply of trained local officials provides a great depth of potentially successful candidates for the elections that will be held over the course of the next decades. What remains is to persuade enough uncommitted voters to identify themselves as Republicans. The goal of the RNC Web site is one way the party has to accomplish that. Of course, to do so successfully, the Republican Party must have a presence on the World Wide Web (and elsewhere on the nets) that is consistently strong, interactive, and attractive to visitors that may not be strongly affiliated to a particular party.

The success of the Republican effort depends on a number of factors. One of these is that the popularity of the Internet will continue to grow. Another is that a continuous long-term effort at party identification will ultimately have greater long-term success than short-term campaign-oriented efforts. And, of course, the Republicans must present their party in a way that users of the Internet find attractive.

The first assumption, that the Internet's popularity will grow, is viewed by most observers of the nets to be true. As the price drops and information becomes easier to find, the use of the Internet continues to grow, and there is no clear end in sight. In fact, the debut of consumer-level Internet related products, such as WebTV from Sony and Magnavox, argues for even faster growth and an even larger audience for political Web sites.

The second assumption, that a long-term effort will be more effective in helping set party identification, certainly has some history to recommend it. This is, after all, the basis for much of the traditional identification with the Democratic Party in the South and in the industrial cities in the U.S. Northeast and Midwest, where the

Democrats have worked for years to have a persistent, low-level, party presence. Their presence, whether it is because of the affiliation of the county sheriff or the block chairman, the frequency of seeing the Democratic Party around has had an impact, but the disappearance of many of these positions, noted by Pournelle, leaves a vacuum that the Republicans can fill. Whether the Internet helps to fill that vacuum remains to be seen, but the net is only one pathway to people's minds, and the Republican Party appears to be working with several such paths.

The final, and ultimately most important, step is whether the philosophy of the party matches that of the users of the nets closely enough to help encourage the party identification that is necessary to create long-term party dominance. Considering that the Republicans, like the Democrats, have a public philosophy that is mostly aimed at the political center, it seems likely that there will be little to object to by users of the Internet.

In fact, the Republican philosophy is sufficiently centrist that President Bill Clinton was able to adopt large portions of it when he ran for reelection. While the willingness of the voters to adopt a party's beliefs ultimately defines the success of a party, it is fairly clear that the Republicans are not facing an insurmountable challenge. It would seem reasonable that if the Democratic president can adopt the Republican positions on many issues in his bid for reelection, then the positions will remain valid for voters looking for a political home.

▶ The Need for Speed

Of course, there is more to winning an election than just political philosophy. In many cases, it is the organization that works the best to get its position out or its workers rallied that prevails. In such situations, the instant communications and reliable transmission of information available on the nets can make a significant difference, especially in the tactical operations of a typical campaign.

One example that may prove to be a defining moment in the history of politics on the nets happened in Massachusetts during the final days of the senatorial campaigns of incumbent Democratic Senator John Kerry and Republican Governor William Weld. One critical event during that election was when the Kerry campaign used the rapid communications of the Internet to offset a series of negative events and to deflate the effects of a critical press conference held by Weld. The result, a rally that was much more heavily attended than expected following a week's worth of ethics allegations, may have helped unstick Kerry's stalled campaign and helped him win the election.

There are other less dramatic examples of rapid communications providing a tactical advantage. When small groups of concerned citizens confront a county board of supervisors, or when a pressure group plans a protest action and coordinates its efforts using the nets, such groups are using the technology of the nets to overcome their lack of size or their limits in funding. The availability of communications then becomes an issue at least as important as any other. For example, sheer size is no longer the only defining factor in the political activities of government.

The advantages of the nets for tactical communications are being learned quickly by a number of organizations. Typically, they are being learned first by groups that do not have access to more traditional means or more traditional media. This is why fringe groups on the right and left have been using the nets for years—it was their only available and reliable means of rapid, inexpensive communications. Those lessons are also being learned by more mainstream groups that have trouble telling their stories through the traditional mainstream media. Therefore, communications through the nets, which do not depend on intermediaries, are growing rapidly.

The lesson is not lost on traditional politics. If there was one single theme that ran through all of the interviews for this book, regardless of the position of the person being interviewed, it was a desire to avoid filtering the traditional media. This distaste for filtering the national media did not depend on the political position of the group or on the ease of access. The Republicans and the Democrats both mentioned the problem with the filtering of their messages as a top concern, despite the fact that both parties have essentially unlimited access to the national media.

▶ The Face of the Future

The trends for the future of politics on the nets are already in place. While it is likely that new trends will emerge as more people use the nets and more organizations try to reach them through that medium, many of those new trends will be outgrowths of practices that have already begun. For the near term, at least, politics on the nets will be extensions of what is already being done.

On the other hand, there will be a much greater use of the nets as a new medium for political thought and activity. New organizations will find that a presence on the nets, especially on the Internet, is necessary if they are to be taken seriously. Existing organizations will find that access to members through the nets will be faster and more reliable than access through any other means. The fight for the hearts of the users of the nets will intensify.

While there will undoubtedly be events on the nets that will surprise even the most seasoned observers, there are still a number of activities and uses that political groups will adopt. They include:

- **Tactical communications.** The ability to get a message to either the membership or the supporters of an organization reliably and immediately cannot be overstated in importance. Time-honored practices, such as precinct organizations and telephone trees, have become obsolete in the face of mailing lists, messaging, and information delivery through the World Wide Web. The nets are already becoming the sure way of getting out critical information accurately and immediately.

- **Organization.** For some groups, the nets are the only medium in which they can organize. Because of the constraints of time and distance, groups with few members spread thinly that in the past could never exist at all can now become viable organizations. Once their members find each other, they can become forces in the political universe, because they can communicate with other groups with similar interests, and because they can communicate with their legislators and with the government in their efforts to get their positions known.

- **Recruitment.** Finding potential voters and members for political organizations is always a time-consuming process. While it will remain so, the availability of the nets as an additional pathway that also provides an easy way to collect basic name and contact information will help many organizations recruit new members or supporters.

- **Fund-raising.** While there are some legal difficulties to raising funds on-line, they are not overwhelming. When political groups are working on the elections at the end of the century, the availability of microbilling (being able to extract small payments on the order of a few cents) and electronic cash equivalents for funds transfer will make political fund-raising significantly easier than it is now. In short, political groups stand to benefit greatly from the same improvements in electronic commerce that will benefit commercial enterprises.

- **Strategic positioning.** A constant presence that users of the nets find interesting and attractive can create use habits that persist. If, for example, users of the nets find that a political party's Web site consistently delivers accurate and reliable information on a subject about which they have interest, they will come back to the site repeatedly, which will eventually help them identify the party itself as being reliable and accurate and bring that person a step closer to identification with the party.

- **Media Relations.** The news media are currently heavy users of the nets. That is unlikely to change, and, in fact, the trend may become more pronounced as media outlets find themselves fighting for a share of a market that is getting more finely divided as new cable television channels debut and as Web sites are looked on as legitimate news outlets. Many organizations have already found that one sure means of getting media attention is through the nets, and many more will find out the same thing.

- **Affinity Connections.** Political organizations are already finding that they can work together if they share members with common interests. While currently it appears that organizations on the left have found this to be more to their advantage than those on the right, this trend is by no means exclusive. Organizations that share common philosophies are already working together, at least to the extent of providing links to each others' Internet sites.

- **International Connections.** As this book was going to press, the international connections between political groups in the United States and elsewhere were fairly limited. This is unlikely to remain, if only because a number of political organizations are being affected by international activities, whether those activities are treaty negotiations, those of international organizations (such as the United Nations), activities from the deliberations of the European Commission, or talks about the expansion of NATO.

Eventually, the nets will provide a medium that encourages both the growth of political organizations that either cannot exist or cannot exist in their new form any other way. However, it will also create an atmosphere in which organizations must compete to be heard in ways that are different from today. While in one sense all organizations compete on the same on-line level, in another they do not. Larger organizations have more money to spend on research, design, and the provision of content, and as the medium gets more crowded, content may provide the defining difference.

In addition, the competition for attention means that small groups that provide only a single voice on the nets will have trouble being heard. To get their voice noticed, many such groups will have to band with others, resulting in a more homogenous message than each would have alone. Does this mean that by joining forces these organizations will by necessity move more toward the center? Perhaps, but it may also mean that some consensus may be found for groups outside the center. This consensus may lead to new political movements, and perhaps new parties that formed their basis on the nets.

Therefore, the end result may be that there will be more groups and that a greater number of views may be involved in helping determine the great debates that will eventually result in policy. Whether that resulting policy is any different than it is now is another matter. There, the result will depend on the tactical abilities of organizations, and that in turn will depend on which groups more completely embrace the technology that makes up the nets.

At present the ability to use technology tactically is spread unevenly. On one hand, many groups make use of the nets for specific activities, such as organizing protests. On the other hand, the major political parties are in the position to use tactical information as a way to determine the outcome of elections. Because it is the outcome of elections that determines how the government works, it is still the major parties that can use tactical communications on the nets to create the political ends that give them legitimacy.

Until smaller parties and organizations can begin using the nets in both strategic and tactical communications, they will remain on the outside of the most important debates, which is the election of candidates to public office. While the smaller organizations will still be able to get their voices heard on specific issues, it is only by using the nets to their full potential that will they become anything more than minor players.

The major political parties are still learning their way on the nets. For the most part, the smaller parties and pressure groups are still learning as well, but a few groups are learning more effectively than others, and if they can leverage their knowledge into a close relationship that helps a party win more elections and get their views turned into governmental action, then they will become part of the political landscape. Otherwise, while their presence will be known and their views heard, there will still be relatively little incentive for the major parties to give them a seat at the table.

▶ The Other Part of the Equation

While actions taken by political parties, pressure groups, and other politically active organizations to embrace the use of the nets can have some effect by themselves, the future of politics on the nets is incomplete without a more significant role by voters. As Jock Gill noted, a large percentage of voters still do not have access to the nets and are therefore unable to receive directly the electronic communications organizations send. For political communication via the nets to be really effective, a larger portion of the voting public must have access to the messages and information available on the nets. Fortunately, this is happening.

During 1996, a number of analysts reported that for the first time, computer sales were greater than television sales, and for most types of access to the nets, a computer is a prerequisite. Also in 1996, consumer access to the World Wide Web without computers became a reality with the introduction of a service called Web-TV that provides a device that allows a regular television set to access the Internet. A similar accessory to the Sega Saturn video game machine allows Internet access. In fact, *Internet World* magazine reported in January 1997 on its Web site devoted to keeping track of such things (http://browserwatch.iworld.com) that the Web-TV and Sega devices were already generating a significant amount of traffic on the Internet, despite the fact that they had been in the hands of consumers for only a few weeks.

At the same time, consumers were being barraged by a vast amount of information about the Internet and commercial services. This information ranged from ubiquitous references to URLs in television commercials to diskettes mailed out promoting America On-Line to news shows on television discussing the Internet and the various ways a person can use it. This constant flow of information, coupled with a much lower barrier to entry through the availability of consumer-level products, is sure to encourage access to the nets by people who even a year earlier would never have considered such an activity.

As the early numbers indicate, consumer interest is already apparent, and consumer products are already being used. This means that a much broader range of voters is now beginning to use the nets, and that in turn means that the breadth and diversity of potential voters the political parties need is already at hand.

This move to consumer-level access to the nets will have a profound influence on the future of politics on the nets. Where once the nets were the domain of the elite (whether intellectual or economic), they are now being opened to use by virtually anyone who can afford a video game or a box for the television set that costs about the same as a VCR. By the congressional off-year elections in 1998, the presence of ordinary voters in political Web sites should be obvious. By 2000, it will be too great to ignore.

A larger, more democratized worldwide net will be an opportunity for parties or organizations to provide content that appeals to the people who will be accessing the nets. Especially as the target users of the nets shift from academic and technical users to consumers, the challenge of content—of the programming and information that people find compelling—is the one that political groups must meet.

Ultimately, the content that attracts the voters, first in small numbers, then in greater masses, will help define how a party or group disseminates its information. Now that the voters can pick what they want to see, they can also choose the content they like best. In a sense, they will get to vote twice, first for the information they like best, then on how the information best fits their beliefs. Finally, the voters will be in a position to communicate in large numbers directly with the people who represent or want to represent them. When this happens, politicians, parties, and other groups must be prepared to listen.

Clearly, as the 1996 elections demonstrated, there are differences between how the various parties and groups listen across the nets to the people they represent or seek to represent. While those differences were probably too small to influence the election in 1996 (except as an organizational tool, as the Kerry campaign in Massachusetts found out), the same won't be true in subsequent years. Soon, enough people will be fully involved in the process that a successful party will have to use the nets by necessity, just as surely as television is a political necessity in 1997.

As the nets become a necessity, political communications will change dramatically. The voters will have a voice that reaches directly to the highest levels of both parties and the government. Voters will be in a better position to hold their representatives accountable. If the nets can bring accountability directly to bear on elected officials, that in turn will significantly change politics forever.

Appendix 1

On-Line Services Where You Can Discuss Politics

There are many places on the Internet and on commercial on-line services where you can carry on a political discussion. These places include the Web sites of some parties and groups, such as the chat area and forums created by the Republican National Committee for its Web site during 1996. Other places include the Newsgroups that are part of Usenet on the Internet. To have access to these News-groups, you need a program called a news reader, which is fre-quently included as part of most Web browsers, such as Netscape Navigator and Microsoft Internet Explorer. The Newsgroups aren't included here because they tend to be extremely dynamic and can appear and disappear in a matter of days (although if you look for groups that start with "alt.politics" you'll certainly find something interesting). The easiest way to find them us to use an Internet search engine such as *Wired Magazine's* HotBot (http://www.hotbot.com) or Digital Equipment Corporation's Altavista (http://www.altavista. com) and search for the item of your specific interest. If you do that, make sure you indicate that you want the search engine to include the Newsgroups. A number of political Web sites include interactive forums; they're listed in Appendix 2.

Here, then, are some places where you can get started discussing pol-itics on line.

America Online
22000 AOL Way
Dulles, Virginia 20166
800/827-6364
http://www.aol.com
Use the Keyword "Politics" to get to the Politics Forum. Once you're there, you have access to a number of discussion groups on political issues, forums, and the like. Getting in to AOL requires special software, but chances are you already have it. If you don't, you can download it from the Web site, or you can call the toll-free number.

CompuServe, Inc.
5000 Arlington Centre Blvd.
Columbus, Ohio 43220
800-848-8990
http://world.compuserve.com
You'll need special software to use CompuServe, and you can get it by calling the toll-free number above or by visiting the Web site. Once you're there, just entering "go politics" using the "go" menu choice will take you to the Political Debate Forum. For a wider range of choices, use the "Find" choice in CompuServe's menus to get everything available on CIS. This leads to dozens of discussions about nearly any phase of politics from the Democrats and Republicans to magazines that cover the topic to discussions of politics in the United Kingdom and elsewhere overseas.

Delphi Internet Services, Inc.
1030 Massachusetts Ave.
Cambridge, Massachusetts 02138
800-544-4005
http://www.delphi.com
You can access much of Delphi's information through its Web site, although most of the best information is reserved for members. You don't need special software, however, and in fact, you can access all of Delphi even if all you have is a dumb terminal. Delphi has a Current Affairs area on the service's main menu that will lead you to discussions about politics itself, as well as the political leanings of Libertarians and Rush Limbaugh's Ditto Heads.

BIX
1030 Massachusetts Ave.
Cambridge, Massachusetts 02138
800-544-4005
http://www.bix.com
BIX is a division of Delphi Internet Services, but it contains a completely separate series of forums (which are called "conferences" on BIX) populated by a different set of users. This is the service on which Jerry Pournelle launched his successful political effort to create a low-cost space launch vehicle. The service was started by *Byte Magazine* in 1984 and as a result is the home of some very technical users, but the areas that aren't taken over by discussions of computer technology are mostly taken over by politics. You don't need special software to use BIX, but there's only a limited amount of access available on the World Wide Web.

The Well
Sausalito, California
http://www.well.com
The Well is considered by many to be the prototypical conferencing system. This service consists of 260 conferences, many of which are political in nature and several of which are specifically about the political process. The Well is well known on the Internet as being one of the birthplaces of on-line activism, and it is one of the areas where Jim Warren got his start.

Netsite: http://www.democrats.org/

at's New?   What's Cool?   Destinations   Net Search   People   Software

Appendix 2

Political Groups on the Internet

Many political organizations make information available on the Internet. The organizations include the major (and many of the minor) political parties, political action groups, committees, study sites, and the like. Campaign site are not included because they vary from month to month. Nonpartisan groups that study politics are included. Of course, political activity and the Internet being what they are, all these addresses can change, so if you can't find one, check your favorite search engine.

http://www.democrats.org
This is the primary site of the Democratic National Committee on the Internet. During campaigns, many Democratic candidates also have Internet sites, many accessible through the DNC Web site.

http://www.rnc.org
This is the Republican National Committee site on the Internet. This site still contains the e-mail addresses and phone numbers of Republican Party officials and the GOP forum popular with Internet users during the 1996 election. Republican candidate sites can be accessed during election years.

http://www.ai.mit.edu/people/msb/ppp/home.html
MIT researcher Mark Bonchek keeps visitors to his political participation home page up to date with his research on the impact of the

Internet on the political process. He also provides information and sources for further study.

http://ksgwww.harvard.edu/
The Kennedy School of Government's page provides access to much of that organization's research on the role of the nets in the functioning of the political proccess.

http://www.conservative-party.org.uk/
The Conservative Party in the United Kingdom has an active site; with the elections in 1997, it should be even more active.

http://www.labour.org.uk/
The Labour Party in the United Kingdom is active in campaigning to reestablish its hold on the government. Even early in 1997, this site was involved in preparing for the upcoming campaign.

http://www.townhall.com/
The page for Conservative politics in the United States. This page includes opinion, media clips, and links to other pages.

http://www.igc.org/igc/
The Institute for Global Communications is the home of Progressive politics on the Internet. This site contains links to Progressive and labor organizations, as well as a number of political issues of interest to the political left.

http://www.iww.org/
The Industrial Workers of the World page includes information on the group's political agenda, as well as links to over a hundred organizations of interest to its members.

http://www.whitehouse.gov/
The White House home page is well known to most users of the Internet. The page now contains links to nearly everything else in the federal government.

http://thomas.loc.gov/
Thomas is a Web page run by the Library of Congress that provides the text and status of bills and other government initiatives, as well as a wealth of background information.

http://www.lp.org/
The Libertarian Party home page contains details about the party's beliefs and practices, as well as links to state parties and information on upcoming activities.

http://www.newparty.org/
The New Party is a small political movement that's using the Internet as a way to increase its effectiveness.

http://www.reformparty.org/
Despite a weak showing in the 1996 elections, Ross Perot's Reform Party is still active on the Internet.

http://www.neosoft.com/~eris/PPPP/
The Pansexual Peace Party is a radical party that believes in peace through elimination of drug laws and increased sexual freedom. The group uses the Internet as a way to spread its message and avoid the traditional media.

http://www.powerpark.com/bmdesign/TCL/
The Conservative Link is a page that specializes in links to other Conservative pages.

http://www.cjnetworks.com/~cubsfan/liberal.html
Turn Left claims to be the Home of Liberalism on the Web. Whether it is or not, this page contains a broad collection of material oriented to the Left. The material includes opinion, humor, and many links.

http://www.nra.org/
The National Rifle Association shows what's possible when an association takes its material to the Internet.

Appendix 3

News Media on the Internet

The Internet contains some sites that are more than just the electronic version of a local newspaper. In addition, many major news outlets have sites on the Web that let you stay up to date more easily and let you search for archival information. This is just a sample of major sites. The complete list would fill its own book, so check a search engine for a more detailed look.

http://www.washingtonpost.com/
The Washington Post is central to the world of the politicians in Washington. The *Post*'s Web site contains limited archival resources and constantly updated material, and you can search for information.

http://www.nytimes.com/
The New York Times is considered by many to be the leading political newspaper in the world. The *Times* on the Web contains the full content of the newspaper, plus it can be delivered by e-mail.

Http://www.msnbc.com/
This joint venture of NBC and Microsoft provides content on cable television channels and on the Internet. The service carries a considerable amount of political coverage (more than NBC itself) and uses well-known NBC personalities.

http://www.Politicsnow.com/
This site is a joint venture of ABC News, *The Washington Post, National Journal, The Los Angeles Times,* and *Newsweek.* Politics-now has become a feature-oriented source for a great deal of political news. It's a primary site for those interested in politics, on or off the nets.

http://uttm.com/
CBS News says the network's site is Up To The Minute (which might explain the URL). You can get CBS news stories and videos on this site, including political coverage.

http://allpolitics.com/
The joint venture of CNN and *Time* magazine has comprehensive political coverage, including stories found elsewhere on the Web.

http://cnn.com/
There's lots of political news on CNN's page, plus there's lots of nonpolitical news.

http://www.c-span.org/
http://www.cspan.com/
These sites contain material from the public service network, and cspan.com also contains links to a number of other news and political sites.

http://foxnews.com/
The Fox News home page, containing stories from the network.

http://abc.com/pi/
Who says politics and news have to be boring? Bill Maher's *Politically Incorrect* show helps keep it in perspective.

http://www.npr.org/news/
You'll find out things about politics on NPR that you'll probably never hear elsewhere. This site includes audio broadcasts of its news programs.

http://www.csmonitor.com/
The *Christian Science Monitor* and its highly regarded outlet Monitor Radio provide an electronic version on this page. Detailed, thoughtful stories and live radio feeds make this a worthwhile site.

http://www.usatoday.com/
The stories may not be long, but the coverage is broad, and the *USA Today* Web site is updated continuously.

http://www.cq.com/
Congressional Quarterly is one of the leading political magazines in Washington. This site keeps you up to date. The site includes a link to a CQ page on Time-Warner's Pathfinder that lets you track congressional voting records.

http://pathfinder.com/
Time-Warner's Pathfinder contains links to a wide variety of news sources that carry political information.

http://npc.press.org/
Virtually everyone who wants to make a splash in Washington speaks (or at least tries to) at the National Press Club. This site also includes links to other media resources.

http://www.enews.com/
The Electronic Newsstand is a guide to a wide variety of magazines, many of which have unique political content.

Http://www.commweek.com/
I'd blush, but all of this contact with politics has made me forget how. Every week in *Communications Week,* you can find my column. Sometimes it's about politics and the nets, sometimes it's not. If you go to this page, look until you find the (cleverly hidden) link to "Opinion" and search from there. You might find it.

ape

View   Go   Bookmarks   Options   Directory   Window   Help

Home   Reload   Open   Print   Find   Stop

etsite http://www.democrats.org/

's New?   What's Cool?   Destinations   Net Search   People   Software

Index

References to Web page images are in italics. A color Web page insert appears between pages 50 and 51.